THE PITCHING BIBLE

The Seven Secrets of a Successful Business Pitch

Paul Boross

The Pitch Doctor

CGW
PUBLISHING

2010

THE PITCHING BIBLE

The Seven Secrets of a Successful Business Pitch

First Edition: September 2010

ISBN 978-0-9565358-2-5

CGW Publishing 2010

Cover design and typesetting by CGW Publishing

Visit www.thepitchdoctor.tv and www.thepitchingbible.com

Published by:

CGW Publishing

PB 1502

PO Box 15113

Birmingham

B2 2NJ

United Kingdom

www.cgwpublishing.com

Contents

Index of Exercises

SECRET 1

IT'S ALL ABOUT THEM

What Do You Mean, It's All About Them?

A pitch requires three basic components; you, an idea and an audience. Without an idea, it's just a conversation. Without you, there's no-one to pitch. If you could get what you need all by yourself, you wouldn't need an audience.

While it's your idea or product that you're pitching, the audience is somehow instrumental in your idea becoming a reality or your product reaching the market.

The first thing to think about when you create your pitch is the audience. Specifically, what you want them to do.

A good place to start developing a skill is to find someone who already has it. It is easy to find people who present themselves well and people who do it badly. Just turn on the TV or radio to find people giving speeches or press conferences, and notice what works best. Notice what you believe, what you trust, what grabs your attention and what makes you reach for the remote control.

We have all seen so many public speakers, starting from when we first went to school, so you already have the knowledge you need to be an outstanding presenter. In your head is a model of excellence that we can draw upon for you to develop your skills. You already know what inspires you – the chances are that it will inspire other people too, because it will already be a natural part of your own personality and communication style.

I was explaining this to my friend, the British TV impressionist Alistair McGowan, who told me that while he had been working on an impression of a professional footballer, Alan Stubbs, he was invited to play in a pro-celebrity charity football match. By his own admission, his football skills generally leave something to be desired, so for fun, during the match, he began to do his impression of Alan

Stubbs while playing. His posture changed along with his perception and he found that he could control the ball and play better than he had ever played in his life. After the game, a retired professional football coach approached Alistair and asked him if he had ever played professionally, or had trials for any clubs in his youth. Alistair was surprised and flattered to discover that he could 'borrow' the talents of a professional footballer, and you can do the same.

Think of someone who, for you, is an exceptional presenter, trainer, teacher or performer. How would you describe them?

When I ask people this question, I hear:

- ☐ Confident

- ☐ Relaxed

- ☐ Entertaining

- ☐ Approachable

- ☐ Relevant

- ☐ Straightforward

- ☐ Knowledgeable

- ☐ In control

I like to be specific, so I ask, "How do you know they are confident, or relaxed, or knowledgeable?" Their answers include:

- ☐ Smile and make eye contact with the whole audience

- ☐ Use a full range of emotions

- ☐ Have a clear outcome

- ☐ Tell stories (thereby demonstrating knowledge)

- ☐ Take control of questions

- ☐ Finish on time or early (tells you they're in control)

For years, presentation skills courses have been trying to get people to emulate these behaviours. Unfortunately, they try to do this by getting course delegates to consciously copy those behaviours, giving them too much to think about and making them even more nervous than when they started.

The approach we're taking here is to develop the attitudes and beliefs that underpin those behaviours, so you won't have to think about them – they will come naturally.

It is vital that you develop your own natural style so that you can more easily connect with the audience. When your client gets a true sense of the real you, they will respond in kind and you will create a firm foundation for an excellent business relationship.

I worked with a nervous presenter at an advertising agency who was having trouble preparing for a big pitch. When I asked him who he regarded as an excellent pitcher, he said that he admired his boss, so I simply said, "Be your boss". His boss had all the same basic resources and equipment as he did, so the only difference between the two of them was knowledge.

According to a radio interview with Paul McCartney, even The Beatles 'borrowed' elements from Motown songs. When their record was released, they were worried that people would notice, but even a familiar chord structure becomes something new when combined with a slightly different melody, lyrics and voices. Therefore, even if two people deliver exactly the same pitch, they will each add their own unique personality and angle to it. Each will make it their own. Just compare original songs and 'cover versions' or original and remade films to see what I mean.

Don't worry, you're not going to have to 'act' like someone else. That's fake. What we're going to achieve is to bring those skills, attributes and qualities fully into your behaviour and fully under your control. You will be the presenter you choose to be.

Mind and Body

Something else that you need to remember when you're preparing and delivering your pitch is that your mind and body are not separate entities; each one affects the other.

'Modern' medicine describes the connections from mind to body like this:

However, if you look in a medical text book like Grey's Anatomy, or if you have the chance to visit Gunther von Hagens' BodyWorlds exhibition, you will see that the reality is more like this:

You are an entire person. Your mind and body are a single system.

The implication of this is that what happens inside your mind directly affects the actions of your body. You can't separate them physically, and you can't separate thoughts and behaviour either.

For example, let's say that you are half way through your pitch when you become aware that someone in the audience looks confused. You say to yourself, "Oh no! They don't understand! I'm not speaking clearly! I knew this would be a problem!"

Your mind creates a fantasy and your body responds by making it real. Your mouth goes dry and you are unable to speak clearly.

When a parent says to a child, "Don't drop that!", the child responds involuntarily to the parent's suggestion and drops whatever they are holding. As the child's mind tries to think about not dropping, the child's hands relax through something called an ideomotor response. Literally, a thought that becomes an unconscious action. The same thing happens when you see someone sucking a lemon and experience your mouth watering, or when you're a passenger in a car and feel yourself pressing down on an imaginary brake pedal.

Your body is an extension of your mind, allowing your thoughts to act upon the world, and your senses feed the results of those actions back into your mind. You are inseparably part of a feedback loop comprising you and the world around you.

In the world of psychology, we call this a 'cybernetic loop'.

1.1 Cybernetic Loop

Think of a time when you felt really bad about yourself. Perhaps you really messed up an important pitch. Maybe you got into trouble at school. Think carefully about what happened and really immerse yourself in the memory.

Now take a moment to pay attention to your body posture. Do you notice any tension in your body? How are you breathing? What are you doing with your hands?

Now sit up straight, shoulders back, chin up, smile and try as hard as you can to remember that experience.

What's different?

Is it harder to remember the 'bad' memory?

This simple exercise demonstrates that your mind and body are connected in a 'cybernetic loop' and that an emotional state is much more than just a feeling or a mood – it is an entire physical, mental and emotional configuration of your mind, body and nervous system.

People talk about a 'red mist' when they're angry, or seeing something with 'fresh eyes' when they have taken a break, or even 'rose tinted spectacles' when they're feeling optimistic.

The way they feel literally changes they way they perceive the world; not only seeing it differently but hearing, feeling, tasting and smelling it differently too.

Conversely, your physical posture affects how you think. Sitting up straight and smiling when you're on the phone changes your attitude which changes your voice tone which changes the other person's response to you.

An emotional state is therefore a unique set-up of your mind and body. To change just one aspect of that set-up changes the whole thing, just like changing one word in a sentence can change the entire supermarket.

Try this exercise too. Just be careful where you do it.

1.2 Change the World

Choose a situation that you are in regularly, such as a team meeting or your journey to work on public transport, where you can compare two instances of the same event.

Read the instructions and carefully imagine the situation, just before you walk into each instance of it.

In the first instance, the people around you are idiots. They are utterly feckless morons. They have nothing better to do with their time. You may know them well or they may be strangers. Either way, you can notice their blank faces and know that absolutely nothing of any value is going on in their minds. Luckily, you are there to save the day. Without you, the whole situation will grind to a halt.

In the second instance, the people around you are exactly like you. Fortunately, they look very different, otherwise you wouldn't be able to tell them apart, but on the inside, they have pretty much the same knowledge, needs, fears and hopes. Individually, one person can achieve a little, but when you just stop for a moment, look around you and really notice, you can be truly amazed at what all these people can achieve together. You can be proud of the part that you play in this and know that everyone around you is counting on you to do your best as much as they each want to do their best.

Now compare your answers to these questions.

How did you feel as you walked into each instance?

How did the other people look to you?

How did you feel about them?

What did you think was going on in their minds?

How did you behave compared to 'normal'?

How did the other people look at you?

What were they thinking as they looked at you?

How did you feel about the outcome of the event?

What would you say you achieved?

The way that you thought about the people around you affected how you appeared to them, which affected what they thought about you, which affected how they appeared to you, which affected how you behaved towards them, which affected how they behaved towards you, which affected the outcome of the situation.

What would be useful things to think about your audience?

- ☐ They're out to get me
- ☐ They're idiots
- ☐ They don't like me
- ☐ They're going to give me a hard time
- ☐ They wouldn't know a good idea if it hit them in the face
- ☐ They've got more money than sense
- ☐ They don't even understand their own business

No? I bet you have heard colleagues say things like this, though. What would be more useful?

- ☐ They're here to listen to me
- ☐ They're just like me
- ☐ I'm not here to be liked, I'm here to get a decision
- ☐ They're going to have a hard time making a decision
- ☐ They see so many pitches, it must be hard for them to recognise something as unique as my idea
- ☐ They're ready to support something they believe in
- ☐ It must be hard to make sense of such a complex business

What difference will your mind set make to the outcome of your pitch? Do you recognise now that this goes far beyond optimism or 'the power of positive thinking'? Through the cybernetic loop, your thoughts become your actions become your results.

To make the most of this:

- ☐ Set an outcome so that you know what result you want
- ☐ Focus on what is under your control so that your actions achieve that result
- ☐ Reinforce the thoughts that lead automatically to those actions

Perception

If you have ever seen an optical illusion, or not been able to find your keys or an important document when it was right in front of you then you have experienced the difference between objective reality and your subjective perception.

Philosophers disagree on this point. One school of thought states that our perception is reality because we project our reality out on to the world. The other school of thought is that our perception merely represents reality, and from this we get the term 'representational system' to mean your senses.

The philosophical debate on the nature of reality goes back thousands of years, and certainly pre-dates our knowledge of things like radio waves and magnetic fields, which gives us perhaps the most compelling evidence in favour of the representational theory.

Since this debate began, we have discovered that bats can navigate in the dark, sharks can detect electric fields in their prey, dogs can hear ultrasound and butterflies can see ultraviolet light. We have built machines and devices that detect these 'extra sensory' signals and shift them into the limited range of our sensory organs.

What we can deduce is that most of what goes on in the world is completely out of our perception, and what little is within our perceptual limits is usually outside of our awareness.

For example, are you aware of the temperature of the air around you? Or the sensation in your feet? Or the weight of the book? Were you aware of these things until I pointed them out to you? What else is outside of your awareness until you focus your attention on it?

Are the horizontal lines curved or straight?[1]

There are two faces at the bottom of the page. Hold the book at arm's length and, with your left eye closed, look directly and only at the left face.

Move the book slowly towards you until the right face disappears. What's happening?

Try closing your right eye and looking at the right face.

---

1   You'll find the solutions to these and other puzzles in the Appendix.

Are these two table tops the same size as each other?

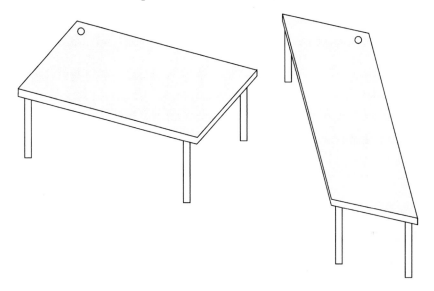

Even a night out at the cinema gives you a chance to experiment with your visual perception.

Look at the stick man at the bottom right of this page. For a start, you are able to perceive a collection of lines as a representation of a man. Secondly, if you flick through the pages of the book, you'll see him move. Logically, you know that the only thing that's moving is the paper as you flick through the pages, but I want you to note how easily and naturally you perceive that the man is moving.

The images don't move on the cinema screen, but the changing pattern of light from one frame to the next gives the illusion of movement as your brain tries to make sense of the information being presented.

This is a very old and important experiment, because it shows that your perception bears little relation to any external, objective reality. The

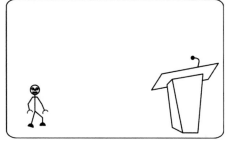

world around you only appears the way that it does because your eyes happen to work that way. The world looks very different to butterflies, dogs or bats.

When you couldn't see your keys, your perception was modified by your belief that you couldn't find your keys. Your brain had to cope with two competing pieces of information; the knowledge that you couldn't find your keys and the visual perception of something that looked a lot like your keys. Rather worryingly, your brain decided that you were right and your eyes were wrong. As Groucho Marx said, "Who are you going to believe, me or your own eyes?"

Ultimately, your eyes aren't seeing words and images, people and places, they only receive patterns of light.

As a baby, you had to learn to distinguish what you could see by using your other senses, mainly touch, to learn how to use your eyes. You had to learn about perspective, shadows and other cues that enable you to know the difference between your keys and the table beneath them. Your brain has to turn raw data into something that you can label as 'keys' and since these perceptual filters stand in the way of that process, your beliefs can get in there first and influence how the world appears. Just don't think for a moment that this is how the world 'is'. (is this a deliberate sentence?)

What would it be like if you could modify your perception with other beliefs? Beliefs such as the knowledge that your pitch is going to be successful, or that you'll easily be aware of very subtle non-verbal signals from the client? Wouldn't that be useful?

How do you think you might set up your perception in this way? That's right; with an outcome. Outcomes focus your attention, and in order to focus your attention, your perceptual filters must be tuned in to whatever you want to focus on.

When you set an outcome to get strong rapport with the audience, and your perception becomes tuned in to the signs of rapport, you achieve your outcome more easily and your pitch is more successful. So you can see, outcomes are more than just goals or results to aim for – they are also the means by which you direct your unconscious mind towards achieving those results.

This is achieved by influencing the way that your perceptual filters work. Simply, there is far too much information in the world around you, so your senses reduce that information so that you can more easily navigate around your environment.

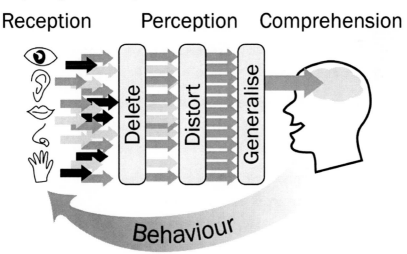

As information arrives from your sensory organs, the first filter simply deletes anything that is not relevant to you. What sounds can you hear around you? When did you become aware of them?

The next filter changes information so that the world appears how you would like it to be. Think about someone at work who really irritates you. When you stop and think about it now, is their voice really as whiny as you imagine it to be?

What about your favourite childhood sweets, are you convinced that they're smaller than they used to be?

People who are afraid of spiders often see them in a distorted way, thinking that they are bigger than they actually are.

The final filter generalises information so that the world fits the rules that you have formed during the course of your life. It also makes sure that, once you have noticed something that gets your attention, you'll carry on noticing it. Like someone's annoying personal habit, or a dripping tap, or that strange noise in your car.

For example, you never put your keys on the kitchen table, so they can't be there. Words such as never, always, everyone, nobody, everywhere and nowhere are generalisations or rules.

People change their experience of the world so that their generalisations remain true, because generalisations are beliefs are rules are truths, and no-one likes to be proven wrong, do they?

By now, you might have realised that these same perceptual processes are going on in everyone around you. When you pitch, your perceptions determine your performance, and part of that is understanding how your audience form their perceptions of you.

For a start, they are deleting most of what's going on. All that effort you put into the details of your pitch will go unnoticed. They're not being dismissive; they just aren't paying attention to anything that isn't on their 'radar'. Unless you draw their attention to it, of course.

Secondly, they're distorting what you say because they have already decided what their opinion is going to be, so they change what they hear so that it reinforces their preconceptions. Unless, of course, you directly challenge those preconceptions.

Finally, they're generalising what you say because it's the same as the last 10 pitches. Unless you find exceptions to those rules and force them to see your pitch in all of its unique splendour, of course.

When the client has 'seen it all before', you're having to overcome those preconceptions before anything that you say or do will make any difference. The client has seen so many pitches that weren't unique that yours has to stand out even more. You may have thought that this was a bad thing, but actually this is a very good thing, and it's one of those counter-intuitive ideas that excellent pitchers take advantage of.

When the audience's attention is so selective, it can be easier to pitch to their preconceptions and selectivity first before opening your pitch out. This is what happens when you first gain relevant rapport before broadening your pitch to convey your key message.

When the client regards the majority of pitches as 'noise', he or she is making it easier for you to make your pitch stand out. When the client has to look carefully at every pitch because he or she can't tell good from bad, they are far more susceptible to influence from even mediocre pitchers. When they have raised their 'sensitivity' to the level where you can tangibly feel their "come on.. impress me" attitude, only the best pitchers get noticed, and by putting into practice what you're learning here, the audience will ignore most of what your competitors have to say without you having to do anything more than raise the quality of your pitch above the level of that background noise.

Bear all of this in mind as you work through this book, because influencing your audience's perceptions is one of the fundamental things that you have to get right in order to pitch successfully, and the Seven Secrets contain the keys for you to achieve just that.

Ready, Aim...

You need to understand, and I mean really, really understand, that most people who pitch for business make a very simple yet damaging mistake when they prepare for a pitch.

This doesn't mean that most people are stupid. Far from it. In light of the first mistake they make, they are absolutely brilliant. It's just that they set themselves up for more hard work than they need to, so the fact that they are still successful at all is down to a significant amount of effort.

The mistake is so subtle that you really can't blame them for it.

Think of the last time that you presented, or pitched, or wrote a proposal document, or in any way communicated with a potential customer with the intention of winning business.

What was your objective?

Now ask your colleagues what their objective is when they pitch.

The chances are that your objective was "to win the business".

That's the first mistake.

What has to happen in order for you to win the business? You just turn up and pitch? If that was the case, you would win every time. Why don't you win every time? Competition? Budget? Something else that was out of your control?

Many pitchers act as if this is the process they have to go through:

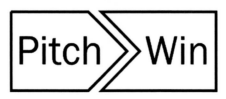

When they lose the pitch, the result is outside of their control. They blame price, competition, a bad day or some other factor. They're not just trying to avoid the blame because they were never in a position to win in the first place.

It's like the 'we woz robbed' approach and blaming the referee for the outcome of a football match. Some fans do, or at least they try to when they question the ref 's visual acuity and parentage.

I do appreciate that this might not be an easy concept to get your head round, but I really do urge you to bear with me, because until you get this fundamental point fixed firmly in your mind, you will never get the maximum return on the time and effort you invest in your pitches.

Think about the last pitch you lost. What reason did you give your colleagues or manager? What was the real reason?

Let's say for the sake of argument that you said you lost on price, and that secretly you think you just didn't do enough to neutralise their price objections before the pitch. Whatever you feel about that, you can at least console yourself that your lack of preparation or groundwork was not the real reason why you lost.

The chances are that you lost, simply, because you set out to win.

"But Paul", I hear you whimper in frustration, "if I don't set out to win, what's the point in pitching?"

Let's draw on an analogy from the world of sales.

Some sales people hate 'cold calling' and will do anything to avoid it. Because they rarely do it, they don't succeed at it.

Some sales people hate 'cold calling' but do it anyway. They focus on the result they want to get and they make it look

very difficult indeed.

Some sales people just get on with 'cold calling' as part of their job. They focus on method, not result, and they make it look very easy, because they know that it is easy. I mean, phoning up strangers and asking for something. How hard can it be?

Let's take a quick look at the attitude and behaviour of people who are good at cold calling and succeed easily compared to those who hit their targets through sheer hard work and desperation.

The Winners	The Strugglers:
☐ Aim for a method	☐ Aim for a result
☐ Work consistently	☐ Work randomly
☐ Focus on calls, not sales	☐ Focus on sales, not calls
☐ Qualify hard	☐ Don't qualify
☐ Value their time	☐ Value not being rejected

Strugglers chase sales, so they will talk to anyone who will listen to them, regardless of whether that person fits the criteria for a customer or not. They are always busy because they are talking to lots of people. Their calls take too long because they like being liked and they can't make as many as they need to because they don't qualify opportunities. They have no idea why their successful calls are successful, and they change what they do each time, always trying to find a new way to close a sale.

Strugglers don't know their call statistics and they have to work hard for every sale. When they do succeed, they often attribute it to luck, timing or to some general trait of theirs such as persistence. They believe that sales is a 'numbers game' and you just have to keep at it.

Remember, Strugglers don't lose, they just have to work so much harder to win, and they tend not to learn from their mistakes.

Winners make calls. They don't aim for a result. They don't try to sell, because they know that selling is dependent on too many factors that are not under their control. They aim for consistency because they understand that if they don't behave in the same way every time, they can never measure how effective they are and they can never improve. By being consistent, Winners can improve. How Winners make calls is completely under their control. What the person on the other end of the telephone says or does is not under the Winner's control.

Winners understand their statistics, so they know exactly how many calls they have to make for every sale. If they have to make 100 calls for every sale, they get on and make 100 calls. They just don't know whether the sale will happen on call one or call 100, so they treat every call the same, as if it is their first of the day. They don't try to control the statistics because they know that the statistics are a reflection of reality.

Winners focus on quickly clearing out the 99 'nos' so that they waste no time in getting to the one 'yes'. A call that ends in a 'no' is an excellent result, because they're one call closer to finding the 'yes'.

Because Winners value their time, they only spend it with someone who is likely to be a customer. Almost the first thing they do on a call is qualify the prospect. This also values the prospect's time.

A Winner understands that they have to drive the sales process, that the decision is outside of their control and that the best way for them to be successful is to constantly measure and improve what they do, and then just get on and do it.

If we step back into the world of pitching – and a cold call is

really a specialised form of pitching – then we can see that the sales process is not the simple two stage sequence that we saw previously:

Relationship >> Pitch >> Decision >> Win

You don't just turn up and pitch to a complete stranger. Whether you have a market stall or a corporate empire, there is some kind of relationship in place that sets the context for the pitch. If someone is in the market square, they are expecting to be pitched to.

The reason that Winners measure everything they do is that their criteria for a great sales call isn't that they felt 'on fire' or they blurted out all of their USPs before the customer hung up, it's that the customer said 'yes'. Whether they happen to agree with a particular approach or not, they judge it by its results.

A Struggler will feel that they have given their best possible pitch and that the decision is now 'in the laps of the Gods'. A Winner will test and measure and get feedback from the customer, and they will give the customer the space to make their minds up.

Both the Winner and Struggler know that the customer's decision is out of their control. The vital difference is that the Struggler is aiming for that decision to be a 'yes', so they will try to influence, coerce and manipulate the decision as much as they can, which is generally counter-productive. The Winner, on the other hand, just wants a decision, yes or no. If it's a 'yes', great. If it's a 'no', just tell me quickly so I can get on to the next call.

The Winner is in control because they are not trying to control, and in Secret Two we'll explore more about winning as an outcome.

Fire!

Once the pitch begins, Winners are no longer thinking about the end result, they are just doing their best.

Where a Struggler's objective for a pitch might be, "To win the business", a Winner's objective would be, "To get the message across as clearly and as strongly as I can, and to make sure that before I leave the room, the audience absolutely understands my proposal and how it is different to my competitors' proposals".

Based on this, a Winner knows exactly what to do once they are standing in front of the audience.

It can be very difficult to give up the need to control the result and, in doing so, realise that you have more control of the result. Very few managers would officially agree with someone who says they didn't mind whether they win or lose, mainly for fear that their manager would think they weren't driving the sales team hard enough.

There's an important difference between letting go of the need to control and not caring about the result. Winners care very much about the result, they just understand that the more they focus on what they control, the more likely they are to influence the result.

Imagine that you are having dinner at a nice restaurant. You would like a glass of water. Assuming that you're not the kind of person to go into the kitchen and help yourself, you have to get someone else to get the water for you.

Getting the water is not under your control, but it is under the waiter's control. The problem is that getting the waiter to do what you want is not under your control either.

Put yourself in this scenario, and then ask yourself which of the following methods you

would use to get some water:

- ☐ Gasp and croak, "water... water..."

- ☐ Pretend to choke on your bread roll

- ☐ Cry because someone on another table has some water

- ☐ Refuse to eat a thing until you get some water

- ☐ Glare at your partner until he/she does something to help

- ☐ Wait until the waiter comes to ask if you are enjoying your meal, but realise that he has timed his question perfectly with you having your mouth full and by the time you have swallowed, he has disappeared again

- ☐ Go to the toilet and drink from the tap

- ☐ Glare at anyone with water so that they feel guilty

- ☐ Distract some diners on another table and steal their water

- ☐ Sneak into the waiter's changing room, put on a waiter's uniform and go into the kitchen to get yourself some water

- ☐ Set off the fire alarm and sit back with your mouth open

- ☐ Focus intently on the waiter and attempt to communicate your thirst telepathically into his mind (If this works, he'll probably just get himself a glass of water!)

- ☐ Call the restaurant from your mobile phone and ask to be put through to the waiter

- ☐ Go round telling the other diners that the waiter has put something in the water

- ☐ Sulk and say that you didn't want any water anyway

- ☐ Wait until the waiter is moving in your direction, raise your hand discreetly and when he comes over, ask for some water

No matter how ridiculous you think some of these methods are, can you see any parallels with the behaviour of anyone in your office? Can you compare them with anything you have ever done when you wanted something that you thought was out of your reach?

Of course you can, because we're talking about human nature.

When people try to control a result that is realistically not under their control, they engage in more and more bizarre behaviours to try to gain control, instead of trusting someone else to help them.

If you imagine, just for a moment, that the audience is trying to help you, how do you approach the pitch differently?

Your client needs information in order to make a decision. They need to know what you want, what your intentions are and why they should choose you over your competitors.

It's not personal. They have to choose someone and they have to make a decision that they believe is right for their business.

If the playing field is level, the only reason that the audience would not choose to work with you is that they don't know that it's a realistic option.

Here are three options for you:

Option A	Option B	Option C

Which would you choose?

You need more information?

OK. All three options give you what you need. They all have pros and cons. On balance, they are much of a muchness. There's really not much to choose between them. If someone said that two of them were no longer available, you would still be happy with the

remaining option. The only thing that makes this a decision is that there are three options.

Now which one do you choose? And more importantly, why?

Later on, we'll be looking in detail at how to tip the balance in your favour when all other factors are equal, but for now, I just want you to understand that, once you are pitching to an audience, you are already on the short list, which means that, on paper, you can give them what they need. This is why I've said that the quality of your pitch is the single biggest factor in the success of your business.

Get Your Focus Right

Ask anyone about the worst presentation they have ever seen, and they will probably tell you:

- ☐ The presenter just read from the slides
- ☐ He didn't interact with the audience
- ☐ She droned on even though no-one was listening

All of these problems arise from the same source. It's also the reason that people become nervous when presenting.

The first and most fundamental mistake that people make when pitching is that they focus on themselves.

You may be thinking, "I always focus on the audience". That's good. Not everyone is able to do that automatically.

Try this quiz out first. When you're pitching, do you:

A	**B**
Think about how you're feeling	Think about how the audience is feeling
Rehearse what you're going to say	Rehearse what the audience is going to do
Focus on your opening line	Focus on your closing line
Think about how you look	Notice how the audience looks
Worry about getting your point across	Wonder how the audience will respond to your point
Think about what you want the audience to know	Think about what you want the audience to do
Focus on what the audience wants from you	Focus on what you want from the audience

If you answered mostly 'A's then your focus is on yourself. If you answered mostly 'B's then you might be saying what you hope your pitches are like as opposed to what they are really like. It's remarkably difficult for us to focus entirely on other people, but a little bit of effort goes a long way.

There isn't a prize for getting this test right. There is only a prize for being honest about where you are right now, and that prize is the ability to master these Seven Secrets and become a more effective,

more influential and more successful pitcher.

As I said earlier, this same root cause contributes both to a fear of public speaking as well as to the collection of behaviours and characteristics that we know as "bad pitching".

Fear

The fear of public speaking is one of the most common problems in the world of business. If fact according to one survey in America, people put it as the number one fear. Here's the list of the top ten fears:fear it more than death.

In fact, according to a survey of the top ten fears in America, death is not very scary at all:

1. Speaking in public

2. Snakes

3. Confined spaces

4. Heights

5. Spiders

6. Death

7. Crowds

8. Public transportation (especially planes)

9. Storms

10. Water (as in drowning rather than drinking)

Now what is surprising to me ,is not necessarily that public speaking is number one, but the fact that that death is only number six!

When Jerry Seinfeld saw this list, he observed that "if this is true, the majority of people at a funeral would rather be in the casket than delivering the eulogy."

When I worked with a group of executives in a well known television channel, I was told that they were all experienced and had delivered countless pitches at the highest level, and my role was simply to polish their performances. When I actually spoke to them about what they wanted to work on and what they felt were the barriers to them raising their performance still further, I was astonished to hear that five out of the six of them said that they were terrified of public speaking. No lack of skill or technique was holding them back; it was simply their fear.

I went back to basics with them and used the exact same principles and techniques that are in this book, because all of the tips and tricks in the world will amount to nothing if they're built on a shaky foundation. Therefore, you must address any fears, doubts or concerns, no matter how small, before you can truly master the art of pitching.

There are many, many techniques that you can learn to overcome any fear of public speaking.

In the face of necessity, to overcome a fear, some people even have a drink or two before getting on an aeroplane. While this can be fine in some cases, I wouldn't recommend it if you're the pilot.

It's just as worrying that some people even try this to help them relax before a big pitch. Big mistake.

You don't need techniques or props. You just need to master the first secret:

It's All About Them.

Change Your Point Of View

If you are a nervous presenter, let's get that out of the way first with a very simple and powerful exercise.

1.3 Change Your Point of View

First, remember a specific time that you presented and felt it went badly for you. If you have developed your current perception since a specific experience, it's a good idea to work with that experience.

Many people remember their first big presentation, or perhaps something at school. When they are asked to prepare a pitch, they mentally re-run that first experience.

It's a fantastic skill, it's just not useful for this particular application. If you mentally re-run a car crash every time your speed creeps above the speed limit and it makes you slow down, that's useful. If you mentally re-run a feeling of achievement and confidence every time you go for a job interview, that's useful. But remembering to be nervous before you pitch? Generally, not useful.

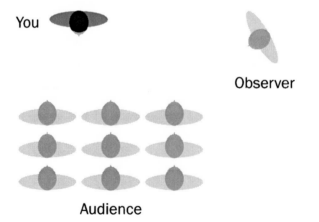

Second, mentally re-run your memory of the presentation as if you're watching a film, viewed through your own eyes.

Relive exactly what you saw, heard and felt.

Remember looking out to the audience, starting just before the presentation starts to go badly and ending just afterwards. Recall the experience in as much detail as you can, making sure you have the sounds and feelings as well as what you saw. Really notice the sound of your voice and the feelings in your mouth and stomach.

In between steps of this exercise, it's a good idea to take a short break. Just think about something else for a moment and then come back to the exercise.

Third, imagine yourself walking into the presentation room and sitting down as a member of the audience. Take a moment to look around you and see the other audience members.

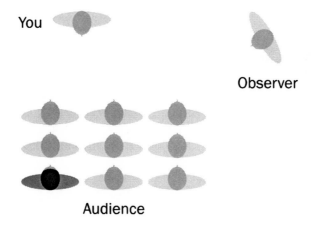

Look to the front of the room and see yourself presenting.

Watch and listen as you see yourself deliver the presentation and run a short film through from this new viewpoint. Pay attention to anything you notice at the point you thought it had "gone wrong".

Notice what you, in the audience, can see and hear. Notice how you feel about it.

Take another short break now. What colours can you see around you? What sounds can you hear? Who was the last person you saw on television?

Fourth, imagine yourself walking past the presentation room and stopping to peer in through the window.

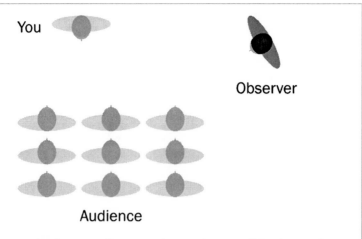

You

Observer

Audience

You can see both yourself presenting and yourself in the audience, and as you look from one to the other, you can see how they relate to each other. As you watch, hearing only muffled sounds, you can run the film of the presentation through again, and notice anything that you want to notice about it. For example, watch yourself presenting and see how the audience respond. Notice anyone in the audience who is nodding or frowning.

Take another short break now. What colour shoes are you wearing? What was the first thing you heard when you woke up this morning?

Now, bring what you've learned from these two new viewpoints back with you as you return to your starting point, standing at the front of the room, delivering the presentation. Run the movie again, and this time pay close attention to how your feelings and perceptions have changed as a result of this new information. Use this new perception to rehearse the next presentation you will deliver, quickly in your mind.

Many people have very common fears when it comes to presenting, and they all stem from a focus on self rather than on the audience. Here are some of the most common things that people tell themselves when they pitch, and some ideas for what to do instead.

Here is a list of some common, natural fears and a simple prescription from The Pitch Doctor for each.

Fears

☑ If you think that people are looking at you then they are. It's why you're there.

☑ If you think that someone doesn't like you, then they probably don't. It's not why you're there.

☑ If you think that you're going to fail, then you probably are, so take steps to change that.

☑ If you think that you're going to be brilliant, remember that you're there to get a decision, not to give a performance.

☑ If you think that you're going to forget what to say, then think about what you want the audience to do.

☑ If you think that people aren't listening, then they're probably not, most of the time. Get their attention, summarise and send a follow up letter.

☑ If you think that the client doesn't like you, then realise they are giving you their time for a reason.

☑ If you think that people are bored, you don't know how they feel just from looking at them.

☑ If you think that people are being critical of you, then they might be, although they probably have more important things to think about.

☑ If you think that you're running out of time, look at the clock!

Welcome to The Seven

Give Yourself A Good Talking To

Some people say that talking to yourself is the first sign of madness. In fact, it's quite normal. We all have the capacity and need to converse with ourselves, as language is one of the ways that we encode information about the world.

From a very early age, we learn to label what we experience through our primary senses. We learn to share those labels in order to communicate our needs.

Language is a complex labelling system that allows us to not only describe things and experiences but also to describe perceptions and relationships. We don't just learn what something is called, we learn to make judgements about it.

It's not just a doggy, it's a nice doggy.

He's not just a boy, he's a naughty boy.

The problem comes later in life when we replay some of those judgements and find ourselves standing in front of an audience with a very dry mouth and a nagging voice saying, "I *told* you were you going to forget what to say".

Guess what? The voice was right. It's usually right. If you know that the voice is usually right, why isn't it helping you by prompting you?

Imagine that voice as a real person, standing next to you. Only you can see them. Half way through your presentation, you realise that you don't know what to say next. What would be more useful for that invisible person to say? "I told you that you'd mess it up!" or "Tell them about the sales figures!"?

The voice is in your head. It can say whatever you want it to say. It's your voice. Or is it?

1.4 Self Criticism

Think of a recent time when something went wrong, and you felt very self critical. Listen carefully to the voice you use to criticise yourself.

Whose voice is it?

What is it saying?

How do you feel about it?

What happens if you answer it?

Try answering it with, "Shut up!" What happens?

Try answering it with, "Thank you." What happens?

Try answering it with, "Thank you. What do you suggest I do differently?" What happens?

Some people advocate that you just tell your inner voice to shut up. Whilst it works for some people, I wouldn't always recommend it. It's your voice, after all, and if you're unkind to yourself, you may just perpetuate the situation.

Imagine that you're involved in a project committee at work and there are people in the group who are bullishly pushing ahead despite some problems that you can foresee. You speak up about the potential problems and they tell you not to be so negative. How do you feel?

Later on, the problems still aren't addressed, so you speak up again and they tell you not to be stupid. How do you feel now?

Over time, the problems don't go away, in fact they get bigger. No-one else wants to

Welcome to The Seven Secrets of

do anything about them, but you feel that you have become a whiny voice in the darkness and no-one is listening.

At what point do you give up and leave them to get on with it and learn the hard way?

If you tell your inner voice to shut up, or if you try to suppress it, the same thing happens. What started out as good advice became a whiny, complaining, nagging stream of criticism. And let's face it, when did you ever like hearing good advice?

When you acknowledge your inner voice, and I do appreciate that this sounds very peculiar, you get the full benefit of it. It's just one way in which your immensely powerful unconscious mind expresses information to you. It's just like your 'gut instinct', only much more specific.

One thing that I briefly mentioned is that if you listen to the critical inner voice, you may find that it's someone else's voice. It might be your father, or your school teacher. Listen carefully to what it is saying to you, and then experiment with changing the voice. Try these for size.

- □ An excitable sports commentator
- □ Your favourite stand-up comedian
- □ A news reader
- □ Someone who you are very, very fond of
- □ A child
- □ A talking dog

What was the effect of changing the voice?

How do you feel now about the criticism? Does it even still feel like criticism?

Practice this, and do it seriously. When you are used to changing your inner voice at will, you can move onto the next, more advanced stage – changing other people's inner voices.

Pay attention to your friends and colleagues, and notice what they say when something that they're doing goes wrong.

"Ohh... I told myself that was going to happen"

"I knew I should have done that sooner"

"I said to myself, if he does that one more time, I'm going to scream"

Do these sound familiar? I'm sure you've heard phrases like this countless times, and not really thought anything of it. Well, I want you to pay close attention to them from now on, because they are literal statements. The person is telling you exactly what their inner voice is saying and, more often than not, they'll even play out that inner voice for you, changing theirs to a whiny, nagging tone or a critical, demeaning tone. They are literally telling you how they speak to themselves.

I bet you can already guess what the next step is – get them to change their voice tone.

You can do this directly, by inviting them to do what you've learned to do for yourself, or indirectly, by getting into a conversation with their inner voice.

For example, let's say that your colleague says, "I told myself that was going to happen", in a scolding tone.

Most people would ignore the 'I told myself' part of the sentence, perhaps answering with, "What happened?" or even trying to make the person feel better with, "Oh, never

Welcome to The Seven Secrets of a Successful Pitch!

mind, it wasn't so bad", in a calm, soothing tone.

If you respond to their criticism by trying to placate them, you're joining their critical game. Sometimes, the purpose of this game is to elicit praise or reassurance from other people. Instead of saying, "I feel nervous", they play out a critical inner voice.

Instead, respond to the "telling" part, for example with, "Well, you do know best, don't you?" in the same scolding tone.

It's a very, very odd thing, but what you're actually doing is responding directly to the part of the person that is being critical, rather than accepting the criticism as true by responding to the person as they appear to you. You are speaking to what's going on inside their minds rather than what's showing on the outside.

Try it out and see what happens.

At this point, you probably have a very good question; why should you help your colleagues like this? Why not just leave them to their own self criticism?

The answer is that the way that your colleagues speak to themselves directly impacts on their ability to support you in your pitch. If you're going to invest time in adopting these Seven Secrets, why would you want other people's doubt and self criticism to be an obstacle. Of course, they'll love the way that they feel differently after a brief conversation with you, so you all win.

Shift Happens

Human beings learn very quickly.

Now, you may have an experience of learning at school which leads you to disagree with that statement.

In fact, most of the time you spent at school was devoted to coding information, not learning new information. Later on, in Secret Six, we'll be discussing learning styles in more depth. For now, just think back to the amount of time you spent practising, repeating, copying and being tested whilst at school. Most of the time you spent at school wasn't devoted to new stuff. It was devoted to you being able to organise and explain what you already knew.

Learning, as in new experiences, happen quickly. As a child, you figured out very quickly what behaviour would result in an ice cream and what would result in a clip round the ear. If you are scared of anything, such as spiders or heights, you learned that very quickly too. You didn't need to spend years copying down notes and sitting exams to prove you didn't like spiders. You saw one, and that was all the learning you needed.

Whenever you change something about yourself, the same process of learning takes place. Some things you learn quickly, some things take a while to 'unlearn'. As an adult, it's not because your old habits are 'deep seated', it's because you have built a lifetime of reasons around them.

I particularly like what Dr Richard Bandler, the genius co-founder of NLP, said about this, "the good thing about the past is that it's over".

Imagine a man who is afraid of public speaking. His mouth dries up, he forgets his words and he just wants to run out of the nearest door. He remembers having to stand up at school and relives the same bad feelings whenever he has to present in his work. However, he sometimes has no choice but to present, and once he has been talking for a few minutes, he is fine.

Analysis, Mr Spock? He's not actually afraid of public

speaking. He's afraid of standing up to speak. Once he's past that bit and has forgotten about it, he's fine. He's basically afraid of being asked, of being put on the spot. Coincidentally, his fear and avoidance of being asked means that he escapes the limelight and the blame that goes with it if the pitch goes wrong.

People learn fears quickly, and they can unlearn them just as quickly. What we first have to get through is the layer of reasons and excuses that keep the fear safe, because of all the fringe benefits it provides.

It's a bit like going on a TV game show where you have to eat live bugs in return for a huge cash prize.

Letting go of fear is often about letting go of the sense of control that it affords, and once you can do that, you can unlearn the reaction you don't want and learn a new one very quickly.

Busy, Busy

I'm sure you, like me, have seen a presenter put up a slide that looked like this.

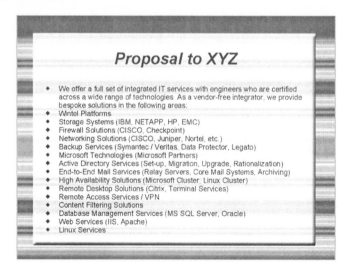

What do you do when you see something like this?

□ Do you sit back, relax and wait for the presenter to work through the information?

□ Do you try in vain to read it and not hear a word the presenter says?

□ Do you get sidetracked, wondering what all the acronyms mean?

□ Do you feel irritated and switch off altogether?

As you read this, do you already have in mind a mental image of the presenter? Have you imagined the way they're speaking?

The problem with a busy slide like this is that it instantly distracts the audience. That may be useful if your intention is to put them into a trance, but in general I would advocate clarity over confusion.

There's another, underlying problem. When you see a slide like this it absolutely guarantees that the presenter's focus is not on the audience.

The intention that led to the creation of such a monstrosity was to cram as much information into the presentation as possible, therefore the presenter is focusing on what they want to say, not on what they want the audience to do.

They think about how much they know and how much they want to impart that to the audience. They think about giving the audience more for their money. They think that value is in quantity, not quality.

The next slide, on the other hand, was created to give the audience what they need to hear.

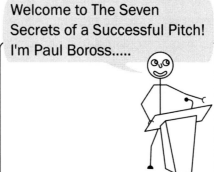

Proposal to XYZ

- ○Reduce cost
  - ○Resources
  - ○People
- ○Increase control
  - ○Management
  - ○Reporting

In order for you to be standing in front of the client, pitching, you must already have met their requirements on paper. Therefore, they don't need to be shown all this information again. The only question that they need answering in the pitch is, "Why should we work with you?"

If anyone will be present at the pitch who hasn't read the proposal then you need to have known that in advance so that you can send them the proposal and make sure that they read it. More on this in Secret Two.

Therefore, if you are using slides in your pitch, review them and notice whether they are written for you or for the audience.

Many presenters use slides as a script, a kind of auto cue. On TV, the viewer can't see the presenter's auto cue. If you want to use slides in this way then, whilst it is not ideal, there isn't a problem with that, just keep them on your laptop screen and don't show them to the audience!

It's All About Me?

It's paradoxical, I know. You're pitching because of what you want, and your aim is to get the audience to do what you want them to do. So how can it be all about them?

The reason for your pitch is you.

The focus for your pitch is the audience.

People who fail generally have this back to front. They think that the audience is the reason for the pitch, and they focus on themselves. They think that they are pitching for the audience's benefit, or because the audience wants them to. They focus on themselves, their performance, their doubts, their fears.

Remember, the reason that you are pitching is because you want something and the audience is your route to achieving it.

It's all about them because that's where your focus needs to be.

When you focus on the audience, you give yourself every chance of success.

Secret Brief

What Do You Mean, It's All About Them?

A pitch requires three basic components; you, an idea and an audience. Without an idea, it's just a conversation. Without you, there's no-one to pitch. If you could get what you need all by yourself, you wouldn't need an audience.

Mind and Body

Your mind and body are not separate entities; each one affects the other. You are a single system, and by changing the state of either your mind or your body, the other follows.

Perception

"Reality leaves a lot to the imagination" *John Lennon*

Ready, Aim...

Winning business is not the intention of your pitch, because that is not under your control.

Fire!

Once the pitch begins, you cannot control the end result. You can only control your behaviour and the decisions you make.

Get Your Focus Right

Most of the problems that you will ever encounter while pitching arise from the same source. It's also the reason that people become nervous when presenting. It's a focus on 'self' rather than 'audience'.

Fear

A fear of public speaking is one of the most common problems in the world of business. According to one survey, people fear it more than death. Fear is easy to overcome, if your focus is right.

Change Your Point Of View

If you are a nervous presenter, this simple and powerful exercise can help. It's also an excellent planning tool.

Give Yourself A Good Talking To

They say that talking to yourself is the first sign of madness. In fact, it's quite normal. We all have the capacity and need to converse with ourselves, and we can make some adjustments so that our internal conversations support our goals.

Shift Happens

Human beings learn very quickly.

Busy, Busy

Busy slides confuse the audience. While that may be your intention, generally it is not useful. Busy slides mean that your focus is on yourself, not your audience.

It's All About Me?

The reason for your pitch is you, the focus is the audience.

People who fail generally have this back to front. They focus on themselves, their performance, their doubts, their fears.

Remember, the reason that you are pitching is because you want something and the audience is your route to achieving it.

Therefore, it's all about them.

SECRET 2

BY THE TIME YOU START
IT'S ALREADY
TOO LATE

When Does the Pitch Begin?

What do you think?

Before you read any further, think this through for yourself.

Answer the question yourself, and ask some of your friends or colleagues what they think.

Hello! I said...

...answer the question

BEFORE you read any further...

OK. What was your answer?

Most people say something like:

- ☐ When you show the first slide
- ☐ When you stand up to speak
- ☐ When you walk into the room
- ☐ When the audience walks into the room

Try this one for size:

The pitch begins the moment the audience buys the ticket.

Think about the last time you went to the theatre or to a comedy club, or even just for a big night out with friends. Did the show begin when the first actor spoke? Or when the music started? Or when you arrived at the theatre? Or when you got in the taxi? Or when you were getting dressed? Or when you were telling your colleagues about your plans for the weekend?

The show began the moment you bought the ticket. When you made that firm commitment, you entered a chain of events that created the sense of anticipation in your mind, and that anticipation laid the foundation for the performance itself.

When you pitch, what is the moment that your audience 'buys the ticket'?

Setting the Scene

The pitch starts the moment the audience buys the ticket, the moment that they make a commitment to being part of the pitch.

From that moment on, everyone involved in the pitch is preparing themselves for it. You are preparing what to say and what you want the audience to do, the audience are preparing what they are going to do.

From the first moment that someone knows they will be on the receiving end of your pitch, they form a mental impression of what that experience is going to be like. They will imagine it being boring, or exciting, or the same as the last 100 pitches they saw, or potentially something unusual. They have already decided how they are going to react to you before they walk in the room.

On top of that, they have already decided how they're going to interact with the other people in the audience.

The hierarchy of relationships is already in place. People already know where they will sit. They already know who is playing 'bad cop' and who is playing 'good cop'. Why? Because this isn't their first pitch.

There is absolutely no point in you trying to second guess this or work out in advance who you need to direct your attention to or who you need the best rapport with, because the odds are not stacked in your favour.

It may not even be obvious who you need to influence in this way, because formal authority in an organisation rarely coincides with the often stronger influence of personal relationships.

Instead of trying to work all of these complexities out, simply set the scene.

When a film directors creates an opening scene, they do not worry about what frame of mind the audience will be in when they walk into the cinema. Even a theatre director doesn't worry about the audience's frame of mind as they come into the theatre.

Theatre and film directors know a number of important things about the audience.

- They are there

- They chose to be there

- They passed through a number of stages in order to get there

- Whatever their frame of mind is, the opening will suspend that and draw them into the production. From that moment on, the director will tell them what their frame of mind is going to be.

What are these stages that the audience passes through? Let's take the cinema as an example.

- You decide to go to the cinema

- You arrive, amidst other people enjoying their night out

- You buy a ticket

- You buy some popcorn

- You look around at the posters

- You listen to the music

- You walk into the screen itself

- You decide where you want to sit to get the best view

- The lights dim

- You hear the 'Pearl & Dean' music

- You watch the adverts

- You watch the trailers for the next film to see

- ☐ You watch and hear the surround sound demonstration

- ☐ You see the film's censorship certificate, which makes you feel special because you're 'allowed' to see the film

- ☐ The film starts

These stages – and there are even more if you really think about it – are not accidental. Every one of them is designed to funnel you more and more into a state of attentive anticipation.

Whatever any individual's frame of mind was before they set off for the cinema, by the time the film starts, they're ready to watch.

This all took place before you saw a single frame of the film.

Just imagine how much is going on before you show your first slide and open your mouth to begin your pitch.

Now, let's look at some of this in more detail and apply it to your pitch.

As You Enter the Theatre

Everything from the posters outside the cinema to the title of the film is designed to get your attention.

The layout of the cinema funnels you past the posters and the popcorn stand, and popcorn is something most people associate strongly with the cinema so they either buy some or talk themselves out of buying some because they're on a diet. In which case, they just have a small tub but promise themselves not to eat all of it.

Someone takes your ticket, tears it in half and directs you to your screen. You feel special. You walk through the rope barrier. You feel even more special because you have been admitted. The ticket even says 'admit one'. You've entered a special place where ordinary people aren't allowed to be; a sacred corridor with dark doors standing as the gateways to mystical realms where reality is suspended for an hour or two. It is a special place with very special rituals; like throwing popcorn all over the floor and tripping over other people's feet.

The screen is dark, other people are in there. In a perfect world, you find a seat in reverent silence, as if you're walking into a church. If anyone speaks, it's irritating. It's against the etiquette of the cinema and, in my view, should be punishable by public flogging!

When the lights dim, it's a signal for everyone to get ready for the show. Your anticipation peaks as the film begins.

When you pitch, what you put in your invitation letter tells the audience what to expect. You do write an invitation letter, don't you? Perhaps you think that because you have been invited to pitch, the audience is in control? No. The audience have given you the opportunity to pitch, and once you take that opportunity, it's yours. They provide the opportunity, you provide the pitch. So, you invite them to your pitch.

That invitation is the ticket.

In the invitation, you might suggest anything that the audience should read or think about prior to the pitch. You might even spell out the purpose of the pitch, just so that the audience is in no doubt about why they're there.

They are not there to criticise. They are not there to hedge their bets. They are not there to drown out your pitch with their own preconceptions. They are there to pay attention and make a decision.

The Lights Dim

In a cinema and theatre, the house lights make sure that the audience can see where they're going. They also play another vital role in that they mark out the start and end of the performance itself. They let the audience know when they can talk amongst themselves and when they have to pay attention.

In your pitch, you may not be able to dim the lights in the room, and if you do, the audience may not associate the same shift in focus, so instead you need to mark out the moment that the audience needs to give you their attention.

Some presenters just start talking, and it takes a few moments before the audience are engaged.

Some presenters start by talking to one person who they do have the attention of and hope that the others join in.

Some presenters politely and meekly interrupt the audience and as if it's OK to begin.

Good pitchers take control of the room from the moment they walk in. The audience don't talk amongst themselves because it's their room and they're in control, they talk amongst themselves only because the presenter permits it, perhaps by saying "It will take just a few moments for us to get ready, so it's OK for you to talk amongst yourselves until we let you know we're ready to begin". Good pitchers therefore hold the audience's attention from the moment they enter the room.

It's not bad, and it would be even better if the presenter was leading the conversation while a colleague set up the laptop. By leading the small talk, the presenter stays in control, and when their colleague says it's time, the presenter leads the audience's attention to the front of the room and the pitch itself begins.

Great pitchers even pause for a moment to allow the audience to clear their minds of any distracting thoughts.

Trailers and Adverts

When people present, they generally leave updates, contact details and so on until the end of the pitch. Why do cinemas show trailers before the film and not afterwards?

On the other hand, why do news readers often end with an amusing 'and finally...' item?

Here is the difference: the cinema needs to sell to you while they have your undivided attention. Trailers are specifically designed with this in mind, and they often feature scenes which aren't even in the film, created specifically to sell the film.

The audience isn't going to wait until after the film and credits have finished to watch the trailers. Similarly, trying to give contact details and other useful information after your pitch just spoils the ending.

News is usually bad. Disasters, politics, crime. News is for people who want to sit down and watch the news. The final item lifts the spirits a little after all that bad news.

I'm guessing that your pitch isn't going to be about bad news, unless it's a pitch to a TV studio about a hard-hitting documentary about bad news.

If you are presenting some kind of project update, by all means have an 'and finally...' item at the end for the audience to look forward to. It could even become your hallmark, so you find some amusing or amazing news item to make sure your audience listens to your regular update with rapt attention throughout.

If you're going to sell, do it while you have the audience's full attention. Do it as you're walking in to the room, as you're setting up your laptop, as you're waiting for the audience to settle down and pay attention. Do it before they start judging your pitch.

I hope that you can understand that a visit to the cinema or theatre is not a random series of events but a process that has been carefully choreographed to capture your attention and lead you on a very predictable journey.

Your pitch must be just as carefully crafted, so let's look at how you might design your pitch.

Setting Out Your Pitch

In order to deliver a pitch, you must have first designed it.

Some people say that they never prepare, that they work best when they present 'off the cuff'.

What does 'off the cuff' actually mean? It actually means that they have written some notes on their shirt cuff. Which means that they prepared.

Their preparation may have taken place over the course of many years, or it may have taken five minutes in the taxi, but one way or another, everyone prepares for a pitch. If you know about it in advance, you prepare for it.

The people who like to appear unprepared are often trying to send a message about their experience. They are almost trying to impress others with their lack of a need for preparation. While other people are sweating over the details, they like to swan in at the last minute and impress everyone with their laid back attitude.

Except their laid back attitude doesn't actually impress. It appears as complacency, and that generally scares the hell out of the person who is held accountable for the success of the pitch.

On top of that, the people who need to make it appear as if they are in control are usually the people who aren't, because they're as nervous as anyone else. If that applies to you then letting your colleagues know that you're nervous puts you in the same boat as them, and they will definitely appreciate it.

I often ask audiences - "Who gets nervous before a pitch?" Generally, about 40-50% of the hands go up. At that point I tell them that there are two types of presenters, those who get nervous and those who are liars! It's all about how we deal with the nerves.

After all, if you're not nervous then it's probably not important for you to win, and if that's the case, why bother pitching?

So let's just clear this out of the way right now. You need to prepare. If you pride yourself on your laid back, turn up and pitch style then you need to take a look at the reality of your situation. The chances are, your colleagues feel nervous when you pitch.

Preparing for the pitch takes a number of important stages, so let's work through them, one by one.

Outcome

Let's begin our pitch design with the most important part – what you want to achieve from your pitch. What you want the result to be. What you want the audience to actually do.

Far too many pitchers say that they want to 'inform the audience' or 'tell them about my idea'.

You need the audience to take action. If it's a decision, then either a yes or a no are preferable to a maybe.

Setting an outcome for your pitch is simple. It's just that most people forget to do it. Delivering the pitch becomes an outcome in itself, and because they focus on that, that's exactly what they get. They deliver the pitch and have absolutely no idea what the audience will do as a result. They shrug their shoulders and say, "It's in the lap of the Gods now".

You'll recognise a statement like this as the hallmark of a Struggler.

On the other hand, many pitchers say, rather dismissively, that their outcome is 'to win', and this isn't useful, either.

For example, you might not aim to win the pitch outright; you might be pitching as part of a consortium for a larger project, so you want to block a competitor with your pitch rather than win it.

If you are not in a leading position, for example if you are pitching against an incumbent competitor, then it may not be realistic to win the business on the basis of your pitch alone. If you have no track record and you know that a competitor that the client has dealt with for years is also in the running, you know that the playing field isn't level.

Of course, the client could be looking for a reason to switch suppliers. Or they could be looking for leverage to get the incumbent supplier to reduce their prices. You know the playing field isn't level, but without more information, you don't know which way it's leaning.

Therefore your outcome shouldn't be to win because you don't know what the rules of the game are. Your outcome should be to 'move the goalposts', to introduce an idea that is so different, it forces the client to stop what they're doing and re-evaluate their position, and that levels the playing field because you have introduced some new rules into the game.

You might be in a position where a client represents bad business. The contract might be unprofitable, or it may pull you in a direction which doesn't support your business plan. In this case, you would generally decline the opportunity to pitch, but perhaps you might want to give new members of your team the opportunity to pitch in a very real environment where they feel the pressure to win but you, secretly, know that it's OK for them to fail. What if they win anyway?

At least then you can decide whether you really want the business or not.

Because most sales people are targeted on sales order value, not margin, they have no incentive to win profitable business. Therefore, a client could stipulate so many bespoke requirements that the cost of service delivery is unreasonably high and the value of the contract is more than consumed by product or service delivery. This makes for bad business, and the bigger the contract value, the worse the problem.

In general, your outcome for a pitch should be to move your business a step forward in your overall business plan or strategy, whatever that may be.

Now that you understand some of the reasons for choosing different outcomes, we can discuss how you can go about setting a specific outcome.

2.1 Setting an Outcome

When you want to set an outcome, ask yourself four questions:

What do I want?

How will the audience help me to get it?

What do I need them to do for me?

What do I need to do in order to achieve that?

That's the simple version. If you really want to go into more depth on the outcome, here are some more questions that you can ask yourself. If you're pitching in a team, you all need to sit down and work through these questions so that you're all singing from the same cliché.

Outcome

- ☑ What do you want?

- ☑ Is it under your control?

- ☑ If it's not, what is under your control?

- ☑ How will you know when you have got it?

- ☑ What will you see?

- ☑ What will you hear?

- ☑ What will you feel?

- ☑ What's the first step towards achieving that?

- ☑ If someone could give you the outcome right now, would you take it?

You can download an outcome checklist from The Pitching Bible website, www.thepitchingbible.com.

These may seem like strange questions, but remember that there are no strange questions, only strange people. Also remember that you can't skip over these questions because you think the answer's obvious. You need to think through each one, and doing that with a colleague is a much more effective way of ensuring that you plan thoroughly.

These carefully designed questions fit a goal setting process that taps into your unconscious ability to focus on and notice opportunities for things that are important to you.

You may already set objectives for yourself, or you might have a sales target and some objectives set by your manager. You might even set goals using the SMART method. These are all fine, yet as you will discover in a few pages' time, they are no substitute for an outcome. A combination of approaches is always good, though.

In general, the problem with objectives and SMART goals is not to do with the goal setting method itself but is more to do with the way that people use the method, in that most people will set goals that are too vague or are outside of their control.

You will recall from Secret One that it is very common for someone preparing a pitch to say that their goal is, "to win the pitch". It sounds fine, and certainly you wouldn't usually expect someone to spend time on a pitch that they couldn't win (although they sometimes do, for some interesting reasons).

The problem with setting out to win a pitch is that:

- ☐ Winning isn't under your control
- ☐ Winning isn't clearly defined
- ☐ The pitch is not in itself the prize

In this situation, you can expect to come away from the pitch with no more idea about what the client's decision will be than when you walked into the room.

Therefore, you need to define precisely what it is you want to win, from whom and what the rules of the game are. The notion of 'winning' carries with it an element of competition. Although you may have competitors, you don't see many Olympic sprinters looking over their shoulders.

If you could 'win' the pitch by yourself then you wouldn't need the client. You can do everything to the best of your ability and still not 'win' because winning is not under your control. If you worry about what your competitors are doing, your focus is on them, not on the client, and the best that you can hope for is to mop up odds and ends of business where you were the cheapest supplier.

In a sales environment, it is very common to spend time on

competitive analysis, and I do agree that this is a vital part of the sales process, it's just not the most important thing for you to think about in planning the pitch itself. Competitive analysis is a vital part of an overall sales campaign, but at the moment you stand up to pitch, what your competitors are doing needs to be out of your mind completely.

When athletes prepare for the Olympics, they do look at what their competitors are doing, because they need to understand what the benchmarks are. But once they step onto the starting line, they don't look back, or sideways. They only look at the finishing line. If they have done their preparation, all that they can do now is deliver their very best performance. Only when the race is run can the judge declare the winner.

When you step into that space at the front of the room, the time for preparation is over. Focus on is your outcome.

Having said that 'winning' is not a particularly useful outcome, you're probably wondering what is?

First, let's find out what is under your control. Assuming that you have done all of the preparation necessary, how about:

☐ Remembering what you're going to say

☐ Feeling relaxed and attentive

☐ Making good eye contact with everyone in the audience

☐ Enjoying yourself

☐ Pausing to think before choosing to answer any question

☐ Speaking in a clear and concise way

☐ Wearing something appropriate to the situation

☐ Being on time

You'll notice that having a good idea or a best selling product is not under your control, because you need the audience to be the judge. All that you can do is present everything that they need in order to make an informed decision. If they agree with you, great. If not, you have to move on to the next pitch.

Somebody, somewhere is going to buy your idea or product. You just don't know who or where or when, and you certainly don't know why. You only know that by pitching consistently and effectively, you give more people more information with which to make better decisions.

When you do your homework and pitch to more people who have needs that are aligned with what you provide, you greatly increase the chances of a favourable decision. No pitch is a 'done deal', and many, many people have snatched defeat from the jaws of victory during the pitch.

By putting all of your effort into the elements of the pitch that are under your control, you are tapping into your absolute maximum potential. Imagine that you are standing in front of a door marked 'Push'. Place your hand across the gap between the door and the door frame and push as hard as you can. Do you expect to get the same result as when your hand is squarely resting on the door?

When you focus on what you can control, you get a bigger result for every ounce of effort you put in. Ultimately, all that you can control during the pitch is yourself.

What about the definition of 'winning'? Ask a hundred people what it means to 'win a pitch' and most will agree that it means to win business as the result of delivering a sales presentation. However, some may think that it means you entered some kind of raffle and won a large patch of muddy grass. Therein lies the problem. It is not only ambiguous, it's not even what you really want.

Later on, we'll talk about the 'elevator pitch', or how to handle a pitch within a very short amount of available time. In this instance, you are giving a mini-pitch that is analogous to the trailer for a film, with the objective being an opportunity to deliver a full pitch. In this case, 'winning the pitch' is perhaps more meaningful, but only just.

More often than not, you are pitching in order to get a favourable decision from the client. You want them to buy your idea or product. Therefore, your objective is not to win the pitch, because you have already won the opportunity to pitch. Instead, your objective is to influence the client's decision.

You're pitching because the client does not have enough information with which to make a decision. If you have submitted a proposal on paper, it's good enough that the customer wants to hear what you have to say about it, but it's not enough for the client to make a decision. If it was, the client would not be wasting their time with pitches. It may surprise you to hear that the client generally has more useful things to do than listen to sales pitches.

There are a few reasons why the client cannot make a decision based solely on your written proposal:

- ☐ They need to ask questions

- ☐ They want to see and hear the proposal, not just read it

- ☐ They need to get a sense of 'you'

- ☐ They have multiple proposals which all seem similar and the only way they can tell them apart is by comparing your personality, passion, conviction and so on

- ☐ They want to find out if they like you and believe you

- ☐ They need to interact with a real human being as part of their decision process

- ☐ They want to know that you really exist

Therefore, for the client to want you to pitch, they are investing in their decision. They want to put a personality to the proposal. What makes the perfect pitch is not what you say but how you convey a sense of yourself.

If you have submitted a written proposal and the client has asked a short list of suppliers to pitch, they are making their decision based on the criteria above, not on the contents of the proposal. Therefore, focus on how you demonstrate those subjective, personal criteria, not on reiterating the facts and figures.

If you haven't submitted any kind of detailed written proposal and the client is getting all of the information they need from your pitch, you do of course need to incorporate the facts and figures. However, as you will discover later on, the audience will not be able to make sense of any facts and figures until they have made the decision to listen to you, and they will make that decision based on the criteria above.

Finally, you don't 'win the pitch' because the pitch is not, in itself, the prize – it is the means. In this case, think of the word 'pitch' in its sporting sense. What would it mean to a sports team or athlete to 'win the pitch'? Perhaps to win control of the pitch or the right to start the game?

The pitch is the surface upon which the teams play out the game, and the rules of the game determine how it is played and who wins, and the judge, referee or umpire is responsible for that decision.

Therefore, the pitch for you is not the prize, it is the arena within which you play the game according to the rules set out by the client.

This is another vital point that most people miss when they pitch. Everyone from budding entrepreneurs to large corporate sales teams makes the same mistake when writing a pitch – they assume that they know what the rules are.

Many, many sales people have walked away from lost pitches, confused because they had the best design, the best product, the best idea or the lowest price.

What they didn't realise was that their strength, the quality of their pitch that they were most proud of, meant nothing to the customer.

Supermarkets offer '3 for 2' deals or 'buy one, get one free'. If you want a carton of fruit juice, the shop assistant might say, "Do you know you can get two for only £1.99?". Yes. I know that. I saw the poster. But I only want one. I can't drink any more than that, no matter how much of a bargain it is.

I recently saw a sign on a supermarket shelf for something that was 30p for one or three for £1!

A restaurant might give you more, because they want to impress you and they think that more is better. True? Not when you're on a diet.. And what happens when you go back and they give you a normal sized portion? Disappointment.

A pack of bacon I bought yesterday had 10 rashers for the price of 8. What am I going to do with the extra two rashers? Make one sandwich? Buy an extra pack to even it up? Put more bacon on a sandwich than I would normally have, which is even less healthy than it was to start with? No, I'd rather have the 8 rashers that make 4 sandwiches and pay less. I just want enough bacon for two meals for two people. No more, and no less. The manufacturer is using the same sales tactic as drug dealers do. Give you a bit for free in the hope that you'll get hooked and have to buy more bacon. They want to turn you into a bacon addict[2].

We want suppliers to give us what we want, not what they want.

Your clients think in exactly the same way that you do. If you take

---

2   In your mind, can you see and hear Homer Simpson? So can I.

the time to understand what the rules of their decision are, you have a better chance of focusing your efforts where they will make the biggest difference.

For example, your client might not care about the range of accessories for your product because they're not in the accessories market, and they don't want to be. You might not do any harm by talking at length about all the great accessories, but you're wasting time that you could be spending on what will have the biggest influence on the decision.

Having said all of this, there are some grey areas, and it is within these grey areas that the most skillful pitchers operate.

The very best pitchers take something that clearly differentiates their idea or product and makes it valuable to the client. When we get onto some of the more advanced pitching skills later in this book, you'll discover how the most successful pitchers find out the client values and attach that to what differentiates their idea or product. They simultaneously get the customer's undivided attention and exclude their competitors from the race.

When you first sit down to design and write your pitch, throughout the preparation process and as you're about to stand up and begin speaking, remind yourself of what it is that you want to achieve. This has to be your primary focus from start to finish, and because your means to achieve that is through the audience. It's all about them, as in Secret One.

Audience

Hopefully, you remember that the audience gives you the means of achieving your outcome. Since I only mentioned it in the last paragraph, if you're forgotten already, you should make yourself some written notes for your next pitch, and you have probably also forgotten about that money I lent you. (Isn't it lucky that I'm here to remind you of these things?!) When we get on to Secret Six you'll understand why this is so important.

At this stage of the planning process, it's time to think about the audience, to understand who they are and why they are there.

Everyone who experiences your pitch does so for a reason. For some it may not seem like a very good reason, but since they all have other things to be getting on with, you can assume that they set aside the time because it is somehow important for them to do so.

Before the pitch, you need to ask the client who will be there. This is a legitimate question and you need not be afraid to ask. In fact, there are a few questions to ask:

Audience

☑ Name

☑ What is their role in the organisation?

☑ What is their role in the decision?

☑ What is their role in the implementation?

☑ What is their relationship to the other people involved in the decision?

☑ If present, how do you need to relate to them?

☑ If not present, how, when and what do you need to communicate to them?

☑ If they have not been involved up until now, what do you need to give them prior to the pitch?

☑ What follow up do they need after the pitch?

You can find an audience checklist to download from The Pitching

Bible website, www.thepitchingbible.com.

Knowing who isn't going to be there is important because if they're involved in the decision, you need to communicate with them. As a minimum, you need to send the 'ticket' and a follow up letter.

If you'll be pitching to someone who has not been involved in the decision up until now, you cannot rely on their colleagues to have told them what they need to know. You need to communicate with them prior to the pitch to make sure that they understand your proposal and that you can build some initial rapport with them. If you don't, they'll be asking questions that could potentially derail your pitch. It would be like watching your favourite film or TV show and having someone repeatedly ask, "Who's he?", "What's she doing?" and "Why are they doing that?".

Having open communication with the audience prior to the pitch is important, and if the client denies you that then you need to question why.

Constraints

How long do you have for the pitch? As a general rule, you should design your pitch to last between a half and three quarters of the time allowed. The worst thing to do is to try and cram as much in as possible. Focus on giving the absolute minimum required for the audience to make a decision. If they want more details, they'll ask.

Where will the pitch be held, and how much control do you have over the environment? If the pitch will take place at the client's offices, can you see the room before the day of the pitch? It's easy to assume that all meeting rooms look the same, but you don't want to arrive and then find you're tripping over video conference equipment or that the room layout is for conferences and there's nowhere to stand so that everyone can comfortably see you.

What facilities and resources are there? Do you need to take a projector, or do they have equipment built into the room? If you're going to use a flip chart or whiteboard, always take your own pens and make sure they work.

Subject

What will the subject be? Does it centre around the product, or the client's problem, or the market opportunity?

Even though you may think that the subject of your pitch is obvious, you can tell the same story in different ways. For example, a film about 'Robin Hood' could actually focus on Robin Hood, Maid Marion, the Sheriff of Nottingham, King John or any of the other main characters of the story. Each would be a film about 'Robin Hood', but the subject would be subtly different and the story would change as a result.

The subject of your pitch might be your product, your company, the client's business problems, or something else. The subject is the main character around which you will build your story.

Angle

What's the 'angle'? Is it how much money the client will save or how much they'll make?

In our 'Robin Hood' example, the angle could be on Robin Hood as a hero, a villain, a saviour, a victim or a myth. The angle could be Robin as a child, witnessing injustice, it could be Robin as an old man, training his new student, or it could be Robin's personal rivalry with the Sheriff as a result of the Sheriff being Robin's real father.

The angle is the perspective of the main character in your story, from which the audience gains an insight into the subject. By choosing the angle, you influence how the audience feels about the subject.

Format

A traditional presentation?

An interactive demonstration?

A video?

The format of the pitch needs to make it as easy as possible for the audience to connect with the content.

Charts and figures would be good for venture capitalists, but perhaps not for creative directors. Product packaging samples might be good for marketing directors but not for technicians. Technical specifications might be good for technicians but not for investors. You get the idea.

No one format is 'better' than another, and certainly some presenters do look for a format which will 'wow' the client, but ultimately you have to remember that you are pitching business ideas to business people, so no matter how much the presentation format gets their attention, what keeps their attention is a solid business case.

Advertisers have, for many years, used the acronym AIDA when designing advertising campaigns:

- Attention – get the person's attention

- Interest – hold their interest

- Decision – get them to make a decision

- Action – get them to take action on that decision

It's certainly worth bearing AIDA in mind when you're designing your pitch.

Structure

Your pitch will tell a story, so you need to decide how you're going to organise the elements of that story.

If you watch BBC's 'Dragon's Den' series, where budding entrepreneurs pitch to investors, you'll see pitches following a number of different formats, for example:

☐ Market opportunity

☐ Product

☐ Investment

☐ Q&A

or

☐ Investment

☐ Product demonstration

☐ Q&A

or

☐ Entertainment

☐ Product

☐ Product demonstration

☐ Investment

☐ Q&A

So you can see that there is no single format that you 'should' follow, only a format that most effectively tells your story and sells your idea or product.

When you plan the structure of your pitch, you also need to consider how you want the audience to feel or react at each stage. For example, at the beginning, do you want them to feel curious? Excited? Amused? Open? Nervous? In Secret Four, we'll explore what you do with these feelings.

Details

Once you have your structure worked out, fill in the details.

If you had started at the beginning and worked forwards at any level of detail, you would probably have run out of time about two thirds of the way through your pitch.

By working on structure first and then adding in the details, you achieve two very important things.

Firstly, you can add in detail where you need it to support your pitch while staying within the time limitations, making your pitch very easy to edit once you start to practice it.

Secondly, you can respond seamlessly on the day of the pitch itself, when the client says, "Oh, I know we said you could have 30 minutes but we have to go to another meeting so could you do your pitch in five minutes?"

As you finalise the details for your pitch, you can create presentation aids such as computer slides and handouts. You can also decide what props you need, such as product samples, charts, models, videos etc.

Computer slides are so commonplace that many people over-rely on them in pitches and presentations.

Opening

How will you open your pitch?

We're not quite ready to open yet, so we'll get to that part in Secret Three. Many people focus on the opening, thinking that a big impression at the start will carry them through.

Unfortunately, there are two problems with this thinking. Firstly, creating an opening that has a different energy or direction to the rest of your pitch breaks rapport and does more harm than good.

Secondly, this approach is all about you, and therefore it doesn't follow Secret One. By putting your focus on yourself and your big opening, your focus is no longer on the audience.

Closing

How will you close your pitch?

You'll find more on closing your pitch in Secret Seven.

For now, we need to concentrate on learning to pitch in the right order. Closing serves three important purposes; it wraps up any loose ends from your pitch, it drives home your main message and it marks the point where you hand the room back to the audience.

Roles

Who is doing what? If you're pitching by yourself, you don't have to do it alone. You have friends and colleagues who can help with the design and practice stages, even if you're the only person to stand up in front of the client.

Once you know who is doing what, you need to brief them so everybody understands, as an absolute minimum:

- ☐ The outcome for the pitch
- ☐ What you are proposing to the client
- ☐ Who you are pitching to
- ☐ Their role and responsibility

When a pitch involves a large project team, it can be tempting to have everyone there in case of questions.

I worked with an advertising agency who were planning to take eight people into their pitch because their client had asked to see everyone involved in the project.

I asked them how they had planned to get everyone into the room, especially as their client was bringing five people. That's a total of 13 people crammed into a board room.

This gives a terrible impression of your company and makes the pitch a shambles.

The Managing Director said he hadn't thought about how to fit everyone into the room. I asked him what he would normally do, and he said, "We normally just shuffle into the room". I asked him how many pitches they had won in the last three months and he said, "None. That's why you're here. If we'd been winning pitches, we wouldn't have contacted you."

What would you have done differently?

You might have insisted on a bigger room, or hired an external venue just for the pitch.

You might have organised the pitch so that different staff were present at different times.

You might have suggested that the client met the whole team over a buffet lunch, but only two or three staff actually delivered the pitch.

These would all be good suggestions.

In the theatre or on TV, the whole production is carefully scripted, with stage directions, so that everyone knows where they are supposed to be and what they are supposed to be doing at any given moment.

My client said, "How come we never thought of this?", and when we treated it as a production and put together a stage plan for everyone to be in the right place at the right time, they won the pitch.

Reviewing your pitches when you're winning is just as important as when you're losing. When you're winning, you have no idea how close you are to losing. You might win the pitch by a mile, or the client might face a very difficult decision. As soon as a win turns to a loss, everyone jumps in to find out what went wrong, and the answer is usually very little, it was just a situation that was getting progressively worse and no-one noticed because no-one cared as long as you were winning.

Send the Ticket

Now it's time to send the ticket. This could just be an agenda, but I recommend that you write a letter of invitation to each person who will be involved in the decision.

Remember that what the client reads before the pitch sets their expectations. When you arrive and see them in the room, they have bought the ticket, they have accepted your invitation and they have a reason to be there.

Practice

Practice until you are confident that you understand your pitch inside out. Do not practice until you think you can dictate the outcome of the pitch, because you have no idea what the audience is going to do and your focus needs to be on the people you are pitching to.

It's also very important, if you're using slides, to know the running order and read ahead of your audience.

If you show the next slide and have to stop and read it yourself in order to know what to say, the audience is already ahead of you. You should have, as a minimum, a running order in front of you so that you know what's coming before the audience does.

'Mental rehearsal' is a technique used by athletes and entertainers as a way of setting a complex activity into their minds as if it were a memory of something they have already done.

It involves using all of your senses and imagining going through the entire experience, seeing, hearing, feeling and even tasting and smelling if those are relevant.

For example, you will feel the floor beneath your feet, feel your muscles move as you look up at the audience, feel your mouth open, hear your voice, feel your smile, see the audience smiling and nodding and feel a comfortable sense of accomplishment as you hear yourself ask, "I'd like to take a few questions from you before I close my pitch".

Do you feel more confident doing something you have never done before or something you can remember doing?

The important thing about mental rehearsal is that you must not imagine the outcome, because to have a mental script for what other people will do means that you're trying to control the outcome.

Racing drivers mentally rehearse a race track but they can't plan for what the other drivers are going to do. Therefore, they rehearse the twists and turns of the track to make it familiar, so that they can concentrate more on the other drivers during the race.

You can mentally rehearse your pitch, but if the client cuts you short, you need to be able to adapt. If all you can do is put in the mental DVD and press 'play', you'll be in a worse position than if you hadn't rehearsed at all.

Mentally rehearsing the client saying, "That's great, we definitely want to buy this", might feel good but it is an attempt to control the outcome, and you can't do that because other people are involved. Instead, focus on your behaviour, your confidence in your pitch and your ability to adapt to the client's needs.

Pitch Design Reminder

Here's a reminder of the stages of pitch design. On the Pitching Bible website www.thepitchingbible.com, you'll find a checklist that you can download and use whenever you're preparing a pitch.

It's easy to slip into complacency and think that you have prepared pitches dozens of time before, so there's no need to be methodical or thorough. So bear in mind that, while you're sitting in the taxi, joking about the way that you can present without any preparation, your competitors are making sure every word, every action, every moment of their pitch is intentioned, planned and practised.

In this book, I'm giving you every chance of succeeding in every pitch you deliver. Don't waste that chance by thinking that you don't need to prepare. If a pitch isn't worth preparing for, it isn't worth delivering.

Design

☑ Outcome   What do want to achieve?

☑ Audience   Who are you pitching to?

☑ Constraints   Time? Space? Resources? Facilities?

☑ Subject   What is the subject of your pitch?

☑ Message   What is the one message you want the
                audience to have firmly in mind?

☑ Format   What is the overall format you have chosen?
                Product demo? Video? Q&A?

☑ Structure   How will you organise your pitch into a journey
                or story? What will the audience's state be?

☑ Angle   What's the angle? Who are you telling the
                story to? Who are you telling it as?

☑ Details   What are the details for the pitch, to fit into the
                structure, given the time constraints?

☑ Opening   How will you open your pitch?

☑ Closing   How will you close your pitch?

☑ Roles   Who is doing what during the pitch? Who is
                responsible and accountable for what?

☑ Send the   Send the audience the invite, the teaser, the
  Ticket   sample, the trailer, 'the ticket'.

☑ Practice   Practice until you understand your pitch

Personal Outcome

In addition to an outcome for each pitch, you can also have a personal outcome which you can achieve, regardless of the actual result of any individual pitch.

Your personal outcome might be something like:

☐ To notice when the audience gives you their full attention

☐ To feel more in control than you did for your last pitch

☐ To learn something valuable that you can use in your next pitch

When you set a personal outcome for yourself, you achieve an overall direction for your pitches that helps you to consistently improve your skills and increase your success rate.

To set a personal outcome, just choose something that would be useful for you and make sure that it fits these four simple criteria:

2.2 Personal Outcome

Positive

The outcome is something that you can achieve rather than something that you want to avoid.

Under your control

Achieving the outcome is under your control, it doesn't rely on anyone else.

Real

You can see, hear and feel the outcome.

Entirely good for you

"If you could have this now, would you take it?"

Was that a 100% yes, or was there any doubt or hesitation?

Tickets Please!

The eager anticipation that you feel just before the curtain goes up or the lights dim is right there, waiting in every audience you pitch to, if you let them know that they're in for a very special experience.

How do you let them know that's what to expect?

Get them to buy a ticket.

Secret Brief

When Does the Pitch Begin?

Your pitch doesn't begin when you say your first word, or when you show your first slide, or even when you walk into the room. Your pitch begins the moment the audience buys the ticket.

What's your ticket?

Setting the Scene

A lot happens before anyone has set foot in a meeting room or clicked on 'File...New...' and your audience is already waiting for you to walk onto their stage.

As You Enter the Theatre

The environment creates its own expectation.

The Lights Dim

When it's time to begin, your audience's attention shifts onto you. This is the moment when you take control of the room.

Trailers and Adverts

Don't launch straight into your pitch. Think about how you can entice the audience to join you on your journey.

Setting Out Your Pitch

When you are ready to design your pitch, follow these steps to make sure you have covered every angle and anticipated as much as possible.

Personal Outcome

As well as an outcome for the pitch itself, you can have a personal outcome which you can achieve, regardless of what the client's decision is.

Tickets Please!

Every audience waits to be enthralled. All they need is a ticket.

SECRET 3

STEADY READY PITCH

Making a Connection

Think about the last phone call you made. What did you do? Did you pick up the phone and say, "Hello, is that Fred?"

Probably not, and not only because you don't know anyone called Fred.

Most people jump to the conversation and forget that first of all, they had to dial a number, wait for the person to answer and then begin speaking. If you have ever been on a communication skills training course, you may have learned that it's also a good idea to ask, "Is it a good time to talk?" before diving in.

The point is that the audience has to be ready to listen before you start speaking.

A mistake that many presenters make is to try to maximise the time they have in front of the client by cramming in as much talking as possible, with the result that the client misses most of what they say.

Have you ever had the experience of someone telling you something and you thinking to yourself, "Why are you telling me this?"

The same thing happens when you launch into your pitch. The client is thinking, "What's going on? Why are they telling us all this?"

Because the situation creates its own expectations, the client will suspend their uncertainty for a while to give you a chance to get your message across in your own unique way. Even their patience has a limit, though.

The pitch is not a race. Time is precious, yet there's no rush.

State

How do you generally feel when you are about to begin a pitch?

- ☐ Excited?

- ☐ Nervous?

- ☐ Apprehensive?

- ☐ Confident?

- ☐ Happy?

Where do these feelings come from?

Do you always remember to feel this way?

Do you imagine how the pitch is going to end before you deliver it?

Do you remember how you learned to feel this way?

Do you remember this diagram?

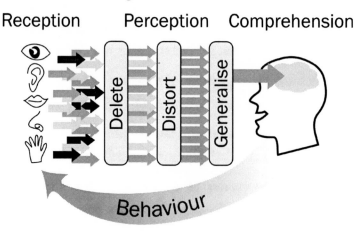

When you first saw it, you might have wondered how it might be possible to influence the perceptual filtering process so that the information that you want to receive gets through.

Your perceptual filter is the window through which you interact with the outside world. We normally act as if our perception *is* the world, rather than a pared down, twisted, simplified representation of it.

We could say that a person's response to external events is a good description for their 'attitude'. Your attitude is the way that you face the world, and it is based on your reactions to your limited perceptions. We could also use the words 'attitude', 'feeling' and 'state' interchangeably in some circumstances.

So if you had a way to control your state, you would control your attitude and you would have more control over external events.

Fortunately, you do have a way to control your state, which means that you have a way to make the world seem more valuable, more welcoming and more helpful than it already is.

Anchoring

Anchoring is the process by which we can attach a stimulus, such as the sound of a piece of music, to a response, such as a particular memory or feeling that it reminds you of.

The usefulness of this process in pitching is twofold. Firstly, you can anchor a state that you find valuable when pitching so that you can easily access it. Secondly, you can anchor the audience so that you can influence how they feel at certain moments during your pitch. We'll explore this application in Secret Four, Dream The Dream.

You may recall that Ivan Pavlov was someone who owned some dogs, and his dogs trained him to keep feeding them while ringing a bell to entertain them. Eventually they only had to start drooling in order to get him to feed them. They could have lived without the bell, but it seemed to make him happy. Whilst this is cited as an experiment in Stimulus-Response, you could also consider it as an early demonstration of anchoring. Pavlov's work, which began in the 1890s, won him a Nobel prize in 1904.

We don't like to think of ourselves as being as easily influenced as animals, so we don't like the term 'conditioned response' yet it's exactly the same principle, and advertisers know this only too well.

In order to understand anchoring, we first have to understand a couple of concepts relating to our emotional state. Firstly, our memories are an important resource in accessing states, and secondly, we respond most strongly to changes in state rather than the state itself. If a state does not move or change, it ebbs away.

When we learn, we associate an external stimulus with a change in state. A loud noise makes you jump and an association is made. You burn your hand on a hot oven and an association is made. An intense emotional experience coincides with a piece of music, a taste or a smell and an association is made. Our entire memory is based on association, as you can test for yourself by noticing how your thoughts link from one to another while daydreaming.

3.1 Making Connections

You might be familiar with the kind of puzzle where you have to change a word from BOAT to FISH, one letter at a time.

In this exercise, start by thinking about your first day at school and for the next two minutes, notice where your thoughts take you, linking from one to the next.

Now look around you and choose an object that you can see. Repeat the exercise, starting with an event that this object reminds you of.

What do you notice about the connections that you have made?

If you prefer, have a friend or colleague make notes as you call out a reminder for each memory that you move to.

Incidentally, can you get from BOAT to FISH, changing only one letter at a time? One solution can be found in the Appendix.

Anchoring is often taught by using a memory of a time when you felt a particular state. What if we anchor a state such as 'excited'?

First, you need to think of a specific time when you felt excited. Once you have something in mind, you need to focus specifically on the moment when you first became excited, because what we need to work with is the trigger.

Think of it this way; if you want to turn a light on, you look for the light switch, not the bulb.

Let's say that the experience you've chosen is opening a present, and the trigger is the moment that your state went from the anticipation of tearing at the wrapping paper to the excitement of seeing that the present was something very, very special. You could imagine the memory as a film strip, and you're looking for the frame that contains the light switch for your excitement.

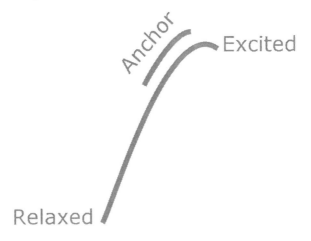

As you run that 'trigger' through your mind a few times and you concentrate on how you feel that sense of excitement, what word comes to mind that seems to represent or encapsulate the feeling? Does it have a colour? A sound? As you repeat the trigger, over and over again, notice how the feeling builds.

It's important that you 'reset' your state so that you can give it a chance to build again, otherwise it will ebb away and won't create a strong association. You can do this by finding a completely different memory to focus on, or by noticing something that brings your attention back to your current surroundings. You could look for seven objects that are coloured yellow, or count the number of lights in the room, for example.

3.2 Anchoring

1. Choose a state that you want to experience

2. Think of a specific time when you felt this way

3. Review the experience and find the trigger moment

4. Replay the trigger moment and build the state

5. Find a word, colour, image, sound etc. that seems to fit the state

6. Break your state by bringing yourself back to your current environment

7. Repeat steps 4 to 6, noticing how the state builds intensity

8. Break state completely

9. Test the anchor by saying the word, imagining the colour, image or sound etc.

Anchoring can have an extremely profound and immediate effect, when you follow the basic steps.

As with any learning process, reinforcement is important. The more you reinforce the anchor, the stronger the association and the more effective it is.

Language is a powerful anchor, and you can easily recall a state with a word. You can say the word to yourself very easily and discretely when you want to access a particular state, and you can have a selection of words and states for different situations.

Whilst anchoring is taught using memories, the process works naturally in real time when we form new memories. You can anchor an audience's current experience, perhaps with a word or colour.

Why not have a word or phrase that you can repeat at specific points during your pitch relating to particular emotional states?

You've now learned a number of ways you can influence your state, and all of these techniques fall into two broad categories; focus of attention and physiology. If you think back to the concept of the 'cybernetic loop' from Secret One, one influences the other. Your focus of attention influences your physiology and vice versa.

The external world, through your senses, influences the way that you feel and respond, and your responses influence the outside world through your actions.

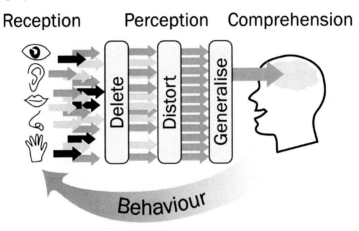

You know that, if you smile while on the telephone, your voice tone changes. You also know that when you feel miserable, other people can see it because you sit and move differently.

To get people to move in their minds – for example, in a learning, sales or negotiation context – it's important to get them to move in their bodies. If a meeting is proving to be hard going, you can suggest that you all get some fresh air and a drink. Get people moving and their minds will move with you.

Many high level, professional negotiators tell me that they rarely make any progress when sat around a table. The time when the negotiation really moves forwards is when they take a break, go for a walk and end up chatting at the coffee machine.

Do not underestimate the importance of physiology, because your mind and body are part of the same system, so getting someone moving on the outside is often the easiest way to get them moving on the inside.

Remember, when you get people to move, shift happens.

Rapport

I was presenting a lecture at the MIPTV television festival in Cannes not long ago, and before the lecture began, I was getting ready back stage and joking with the crew. I find it's always good to build rapport with the people who are going to help make your pitch a success.

Some of the door staff were there too, listening in, and then as my lecture was about to begin, they were talking at the main door.

A friend of mine came to the lecture, and afterwards he said to me, "I had no idea you were presenting today, but as I walked past the door I heard the girls say, "Oh you should come in and watch this, it's going to be really good, this guy is really funny", and so that made me come into the lecture, and I was surprised to find it was you!"

The door staff had never seen my lecture, but based on their experience of rapport back stage, they were inadvertently enticing people in to the auditorium.

Rapport is the invisible connection between two people; a communications medium through which you can convey your thoughts, ideas, intentions, hopes, dreams and fears.

In fact, we are such good communicators that, whether we like it or not, we are screaming our intentions at other people. There only needs to be a subtle connection, a tiny amount of rapport, and that message gets through.

This is why pitching something that you don't believe in is often fruitless. Your whole being will communicate your real feelings, even if the audience can't quite figure out why you're not being sincere.

Rapport isn't a tangible thing in itself, even though the word is a noun and is therefore a thing to be possessed. We could perhaps describe it as a quality of a relationship, like honesty or dishonesty, trust or mistrust.

We can observe rapport by its symptoms, when we notice a causal link between the behaviour of two or more people.

For example, when one person takes a drink and the person they're talking to does so at the same time, and you observe this happening a number of times, you can infer the presence of rapport.

If one person smiles sheepishly while the other crosses their arms and frowns, you can infer the absence of rapport, although you also have to consider the possibility that this is a perfect relationship

A few years ago, I was delivering a lecture in Russia and, as I looked out at the people in the audience, they glared back at me. During a break, I asked someone about this and they replied, "Yes, Russian face always look angry[3]". Some people have said that, because of their political heritage, they don't like to show when they're enjoying something, but whatever the reason behind it, I realised that their facial expressions had nothing to do with the quality of my lecture or the value they were getting from it.

You could think of rapport as being a conduit for effective communication. Without it, it's very difficult to engage the processes

3   Did you just read that in the voice of a James Bond villain?

of agreement and compliance. In other words, people are more likely to do what you want if they like you. Having said that, and assuming that you're a naturally likeable and gregarious person, there are still many things that people do to stifle natural rapport.

The most common is the placing of barriers between people. A lectern blocks the audience's view of a presenter and restricts the flow of non-verbal information - a key component in establishing rapport. Without rapport, the audience loses interest, the speaker gets nervous and the relationship descends in a spiral of infectious states.

A desk blocks your view of an interviewer, so you feel nervous in the interview. A partition in an office blocks your view of your colleagues, so you don't communicate as well as in an open office.

In most situations, it is more useful to have rapport than not.

Since the 1970s, a lot of sales and management training has included 'body language', which is a phrase coined by the Australian psychologist Allan Pease in his book of the same name.

Pease attributed specific meanings to different gestures, and sales trainers seized the opportunity to teach sales people how to fake sincerity and hide arrogance.

I worked with a client whose CEO was present at every pitch they delivered. They asked for my help because they hadn't won a pitch in three months, and whilst things were looking grim, nothing looked quite as grim as their CEO. In his dishevelled, ill fitting suit, he wasn't exactly an ideal ambassador for his company. When he pitched, he shuffled, sweated and grinned – he had all the sincerity of a tap dancer's smile .

Every part of the CEO reeked falseness, and when I spoke to his clients after his pitch, they said that they didn't believe what he said, it just didn't ring true for them.

One of the things I did with him was to get him to talk about his children, a subject that he was very sincere about. When he did that, his whole demeanour changed, he stopped sweating and he lost his false and forced smile. While he was thinking about his children, I told him to deliver his pitch and suddenly he came across as sincere and believable.

Not long after 'body language' came into our language, sales trainers began teaching 'matching' and 'mirroring'.

If you observe two people in rapport, you'll see them moving to the same rhythm, as if they are dancing to music that only they can hear.

Matching and mirroring seem to replicate this, so by copying someone's movements, you potentially create or accelerate rapport with them.

Bear in mind that matching is not rapport, it is merely one symptom of rapport. To confuse the two would be like saying you have a cold, just because you pretend to sneeze.

If you're trying to get out of a pitch at work, pretending to sneeze might be convincing enough, but when you're in rapport, other people can tell if you're faking it. It comes across as insincere and manipulative.

Many people ask about the difference between matching and mirroring. Simply, if the person you're facing raises his right hand, raising your right hand is matching and raising your left hand is mirroring. As far as I can tell, there is no particular reason to do one or the other, so I'll just use the word 'matching' from now on.

It's usually quite easy to spot someone who has just learned to match – they tend to copy you like an irritating mime artist (are there any other kind?!). This does not do anything to build rapport, although it does give you an opportunity to have some fun with them by finding out how far you can go and still have them copy you.

On the other hand, I have been in situations where I noticed myself doing something like spinning a pen in my hand, only to see that my client was doing the same thing. I became quite self conscious because it seemed so obvious, even though I was completely unaware of it.

3.3 Testing Rapport

Find a partner who can help you for 20 minutes with this exercise.

First, find four conversation subjects, two that you broadly agree on and two that you disagree on. For example, you might choose topics such as sport, films, cooking, politics or foreign travel.

Sit comfortably, facing each other with a full view of each others' body posture. Don't have anything like a table between you.

Notice how your partner is sitting so that you can adjust your posture to match or mismatch theirs when necessary. For example, notice where their arms and legs are, where their feet are pointing, how their hands are resting, the angle of their head and shoulders, their facial expression and their angle in the chair.

This exercise is in four stages, each one taking five minutes. Adjust your posture and then begin a conversation on the chosen subject.

1. Match posture, agree on the subject

2. Mismatch posture, disagree on the subject

3. Mismatch posture, agree on the subject

4. Match posture, disagree on the subject

At the end of each stage, note how you both feel about each other and the subject.

At the end of the whole exercise, note how you both feel overall and what you each noticed.

Did you notice that, when you were mismatching, you found things to disagree about, even for a subject that you thought you agreed on? And did you find that, for a subject that you disagree on, you found a different point of view when you matched postures?

Even such a staged and obvious way of imitating rapport has a tangible effect. You both knew that it was an exercise, not a real relationship, and you both knew that the conditions were being controlled. Yet the four stages still had a real effect on your nervous system and your reactions.

My advice is that if you have natural rapport with someone, you don't have to give a second thought to matching. You'll get natural rapport by having a sincere interest in them. When that interest is reciprocated, you will both change your state to converge on a common understanding.

Whilst agreement builds rapport, being in rapport with someone definitely does not mean that you automatically agree with them, and it doesn't mean that they will automatically agree with you. At best, it means that you both become open to other points of view, and that in itself is extremely valuable in a pitch.

In normal, everyday conversations, you can observe people naturally matching and mismatching each other to indicate agreement or disagreement. Watch a debate at work and notice that when someone is talking to their manager, they might automatically match when their manager is agreeing with them, and then suddenly fold their arms, shake their heads, look down and and frown if their manager disagrees.

3.4 The Dance of Rapport

After you have spent some time observing your colleagues, you will probably notice that some of them show their feelings much more readily than others. When people agree with them, they match and reinforce that agreement, when people disagree they mismatch very strongly, almost trying to make the other person feel bad for not agreeing with them.

Choose one of these people, and next time you're in a meeting or conversation with them, play devil's advocate. Switch between two opposing points of view as if weighing up the options and notice the dance that they perform for you as they alternate between trying to make you feel good for agreeing with them and bad for disagreeing with them. End by leaning towards agreement and then saying that you can't make your mind up.

Group Rapport

Another question that I'm often asked is, "Why are you following me?", but frankly, that's not something I want to go into right now, especially as nothing was ever proven in court. A more relevant question is, "How do I get rapport with a group?"

The simplest answer is don't bother. If you are congruent and open, you will find that a group or audience gradually gets into rapport with you. Their states will converge on yours, with more influential people in the group, rapport leaders, moving first.

Don't try to plan this, as the rapport in even the same group will change form one situation to the next.

You might be familiar with the experience of getting the audience 'on your side' and you may also notice the moment when that happens. What you can start to notice is what exactly you do that makes that change happen. When the audience's state shifts, what did you do that made it shift?

There is a danger in group rapport, which is that a careless presenter can easily be drawn into the crowd and lose control of the room. A presenter who is both nervous and who needs to be liked will seek acceptance by the group and can lose direction as a result.

Even I've succumbed to this, when, years ago, I made a joke that turned out to have a rather inappropriate connotation for the person that I was working with. Having group rapport allowed me to get through the embarrassment, but it would have been very easy to join in with the group's laughter and alienate the person concerned, and I've certainly seen that happen in various training courses and presentations. While it might be acceptable for a particular group of colleagues to single someone out as the butt of their jokes, no presenter should ever join in.

As a pitcher, it is not your job to be liked. It is your job to get your message across.

Rapport is a very good indicator of group compliance and you will find that when you raise subjects which are contentious or engage opinion, the audience fragments into smaller groups. Pay attention to who shifts first and who follows them and you will learn everything you need to know about the hierarchical power structure of the group.

Most of the time, we get into and out of rapport with people unconsciously, so our beliefs and thoughts are revealed non-verbally, regardless of our efforts to hide our true feelings. Regardless of what people say, they will show you who and what they agree and disagree with.

If there's one useful thing you can learn about rapport, it's that you can choose the people you want to get into rapport with. While many people teach how to have more rapport, what is probably more valuable is learning to manage the depth of rapport.

I'm Sorry, I'm Losing You

What happens if you lose rapport during your pitch?

☐ Do you stumble on and hope for the best?

☐ Do you do something to get the audience's attention?

☐ Do you stop?

I'm sure we've all been there at some point. One person starts to yawn or gets his mobile phone out, then someone else starts doodling and showing something to the person next to her, and before you know it, you're thinking more about what they're doing than about what you're doing.

Probably the worst thing to do is notice it and then carry on as if it's not happening but worry about it anyway. You need to either deal with it internally by putting it out of your mind or deal with it externally in some way.

How you deal with it is very much down to your personality, and nothing else. How you deal with it is not about what's appropriate for the audience or right for that client, it's all down to how comfortable you are in dealing with people who are being disrespectful to you. After all, would you ask a misbehaving child how to deal with their behaviour? Just imagine the conversation...

"Now Johnny, I know it was you that broke the window, so you tell me how I should punish you."

"I think more sweets should do it."

"OK, here are some sweets. Have some money too. I hope you've learned your lesson."

Emergencies will no doubt arise at some point during a pitch, but if someone gets a genuinely important message, they can leave the room to deal with it, especially if you give them permission to do that at the start of your pitch, as we talked about earlier.

What often happens is that the presenter gives the audience a little leeway. When the first person gets their mobile out, they ignore it. They ignore the second and third instance too. Then, when half the audience are in a world of their own, the presenter starts to think they should say something. Of course, by then, they have implied, through their inaction, that it's perfectly acceptable for the audience to text their friends during your pitch. You need to decide if it's acceptable or not before you begin, and tell the audience, and deal with the issue as soon as it arises because, no matter how uncomfortable that seems, it is far easier than trying to deal with it too late, or not at all and losing the business.

Remember – every person in the audience bought a ticket. They all made a decision to be there. They all knew what was required of them. Any behaviour to the contrary is an attempt on their part to gain control, and that is the thing that you must never give the audience until you are good and ready and it's on your terms.

You've had long enough to think about it now. What do you say to someone who gets their mobile phone or laptop out during your pitch? What do you do when someone starts obviously staring out of the window or distracting others during your pitch?

When someone disengages from your pitch, they are no longer in the room. If they are not important in the decision then that's not too bad, but you must then ask why they are there in the first place. If they distract others, then that's very bad because your tolerance of their behaviour will drain your credibility faster than if you wore a curly red wig, large red shoes, a big red nose and a spinning bow tie.

Therefore, like it or not, you have to deal with it.

Here are some suggestions for what you could do and say. Which, if any, you choose to try out depends only on your personality.

1. Stop talking and stare at the offender until they become very aware that everyone is looking at them, wondering what they're up to.

2. Copy their behaviour. Get your own mobile out and start texting someone.

3. Make a joke, saying, "Don't be shy, you can ask me a question directly, there's no need to do it by text ".

4. Say, "Please leave the room".

5. Say, "Do you need a moment to take care of something?"

6. Say, "What the hell do you think you're doing, you disrespectful ignoramus?"

7. Say, "I'm sorry, am I disturbing you?"

8. Say, "If you've got something interesting to say, why don't you share it with all of us?"

9. Stop talking, mid sentence, and walk out.

10. Pause and, when they look at you, smile and say, "It's OK, we can wait".

11. Say, "Is it too much to ask for you to pay attention for just twenty minutes?"

12. Say, "You're obviously very busy so I'll keep this short"

13. Say, "If this is a bad time for you, why don't we reschedule this for when you're less busy?"

You're probably not keen on any of those options. Most people would think that number 5 was the least confrontational. Many of them are far more confrontational than most people would even consider, and most people would prefer not to have to deal with it at all.

If you don't want to deal with it when it happens, you leave yourself two realistic choices. Firstly, ignore it and hope for the best. Secondly, pre-empt it by marking out your territory before you begin, although that means that you absolutely have to confront the behaviour if it still happens. By pre-empting it, you make it far easier to deal with it.

When you make a pre-emptive announcement as you begin your pitch, anyone who routinely behaves in this way during meetings will think that you're talking to them and, mostly, they will then be on their best behaviour.

Some people have such a childish need for control that they will behave disrespectfully no matter what you do, so you have to weigh up in advance what your options are and how you will handle a problem, should one arise.

The rest of the audience will judge you on how you handle such a challenge to your authority.

Most of the time, the person who gets their mobile or laptop out is also the person who talks over his or her colleagues, 'tunes out' during meetings and gets upset when their colleagues disagree with them. In short, they demand attention and control and their colleagues give in to them. Some people behave in this way to create a false sense of authority. They demand respect rather than earn it and you have to be clear on how you're going to handle that.

When you demonstrate the self respect that it takes to maintain control during your pitch, you gain more respect from the other people in the room, and that is a good thing.

The alternative is that you let them walk all over you and, if you win the business anyway, how are you going to feel about that? How are you going to feel about what you had to do to win the pitch?

The best way to deal with anything is to anticipate it. Having to figure out what to do, reactively, means you're not in control.

When I'm training, I pre-empt interruptions by starting with something like this:

"I know that you are all busy and that you have many demands on your time. I also know that you are here right now because at this moment, this is the most important place for you to be. When we take a break I will tell you the time that I will restart. If you're not back in time I will presume that at that moment, you have something more important that you need to do, and that's OK with me. If you get a message and it's something that you need to take care of, please go and take care of it immediately. I don't want you to sit there, worrying about it and wondering when the next break will be. Just go and take care of it right away so that it's dealt with and you can put it out of your mind completely. I want to make sure that when you're out of the room it's because you have to do something that is more important for you so that when you're in the room you can be 100% focussed on what we're working on here."

How could you say something like that at the start of your pitch?

How about this:

"In a moment we're going to begin our pitch, so I just wanted to let you know that I appreciate you're busy, and during the 20 minutes we're going to be speaking, I'm asking you for your undivided attention, and in return we're going to stick to what is most relevant and important to you, based on the information you have given us. If you get an urgent message that you need to take care of, feel free to go and do that so that it's out of your mind and when you're here in the room, you're as fully focused on this as we are."

Influence

Rapport is a two way communication process. You signal your state of mind to other people and they signal theirs back to you.

Many books have been written on the subject of influence, and one of the most important universal truths is that in order to influence someone, you must be in some kind of relationship with them. The more rapport there is, the stronger the connection and the easier it is to influence.

And therein lies the problem. While you're influencing them, they're also influencing you.

Worse still, if you're so wrapped up in yourself that you have forgotten Secret One, you won't even realise that they're influencing you, and that puts them in control.

Therefore there is no point in trying to use rapport to get someone to do something against their will, because if they feel uncomfortable, they're quite likely to make you feel uncomfortable too. And if you cut yourself off from them, there's no rapport, no relationship and no influence.

When you genuinely believe that a business relationship will be mutually beneficial, rapport and influence will never be a problem for you.

Territory

Good presenters begin by marking out their territory as they enter the room.

Perhaps you've noticed when someone walks into a meeting room and makes an exaggerated gesture of putting their bag or briefcase on the desk. This is rather an obvious and clumsy way of marking out territory, and it generally suggests that the person thinks they are more important than they actually are. They walk in as if they own the place. Ironically, people who do own the place don't act as if they own the place. Do you walk into your own home as if you own the place? Of course not. Therefore, people only lay claim to territory that they know isn't theirs.

What I'm talking about is something far more subtle.

When you walk into a meeting room, you have a right to be there, and you have earned that right fair and square. You didn't trick your way past the security guard. You didn't drug the real presenter and take his or her place at the last minute. You didn't climb up the fire escape and sneak in through the window.

3.5 The Pitching Space

Get a few colleagues together and try this experiment.

Go into a presentation room in your office and tell them that there's going to be a 5 minute presentation that you want their feedback on. This will get them to sit as if they expect someone to present. Sit with them as a member of the 'audience'.

What happens?

How do they interact with each other?

More importantly, how do they interact with the empty space at the front of the room?

The presence of an audience gives you the right to present, and when the audience implicitly hands the room over to you, they are handing you both control of that space and also their expectation that you will accept that control.

Presenters who dodge around at the front of the room, who back away from the audience and who hide behind lecterns and flip chart stands gain no respect from the audience. It's as if the audience threw them a hot potato and they do their best to get rid of it. Since they don't want control of the space, the audience ultimately takes it back.

It is vital that you are ready to accept control of the presentation space, and that you only hand it back when you are ready to do so, on your terms. We'll explore how you do this in Secret Seven.

A presentation room without a presenter is like a living room with the TV switched off. Everyone looks at it anyway, hoping that something interesting will happen.

3.6 Claiming the Space

If your colleagues are willing to indulge your experiment for a few minutes longer, here's part two.

Go and stand at the front of the room, in the presenter's space, but say and do nothing. Just look at the audience.

Stay there for much longer than feels comfortable and notice how you feel, then sit down and ask your colleagues how they felt.

Notice how their comments relate to their uncertainty about who was in control.

What can you deduce from this experiment?

An audience creates the demand for a presenter. When you go to the cinema, you allow the Director of the film to take control of your emotions. You know it's not real, so you don't expect to suffer any lasting harm from the experience.

When people sit in a room and face a screen or even an empty space, they look for someone to give control to. They search for someone to listen to, to learn from.

Maybe it's an innate thing, maybe it's a behaviour we learned at school, I don't know.

For this to be a learned behaviour would mean that people would respond to a presenter in the same way that they learned to respond to a teacher at school, and in fact we can observe exactly that taking place. The more the situation feels like 'learning', the more some people behave like school children.

Behaviours that you can observe include:

- Being teacher's pet, sitting at the front, taking copious notes, asking questions and not having a clue what's really going on

- Being the rebel, sitting at the back of the room, sniggering and trying to draw other people's attention away from the presenter

- Being the class know-all, trying to correct the presenter because they know better

- Being the class idiot, acting dumb because they fear they are

- Being the class clown, joking to draw attention away from their lack of understanding

- Being the class supervisor, disapproving of their colleagues' behaviour

- Being the class swot, writing everything down, asking questions, listening intently, not interacting with their colleagues

3.7 Class Wars

Which of these behaviours have you observed?

Which have you engaged in?

As a presenter, how do you respond to them?

Find some colleagues who have experience of presenting and ask them the same questions.

What can you learn about how to deal with disruptive people?

What about people who are hard to deal with because they seem so nice and helpful (the teacher's pet), when in fact they're potentially the most disruptive?

I worked with a client who was having trouble controlling audiences, and I asked him if he had a teacher at school who was good at keeping an unruly class on track. He said that he had one teacher who would calmly look at the class with an expression that said, "I've got all day, it's your own time you're wasting". Do be careful with this, as the last thing you need is for the audience to make you their teacher because you really are drawn into their game if that happens.

What I have noticed is that these behaviours emerge most often when companies have:

□ Relatively young staff

□ Presentation rooms arranged with chairs and tables in rows

□ Frequent training, usually as a result of operating in a regulated sales environment

□ Competitive cultures

□ Managers who act like parents or teachers

Of course, when one person starts to act out their school role, others join in with their learned responses. When the class clown makes a joke, the rebel tunes out, the supervisor 'tuts' disapprovingly and the teacher's pet tries to please the presenter and grab all the attention for themselves while their colleagues are fighting amongst themselves. The class idiot, rather than be told they are dumb, takes control and puts themselves at the bottom of the class.

Interestingly, the 'Mexican wave' of behaviour is a sign of rapport. It is a sign that the group is acting with some kind of social cohesion. You have walked into a scenario that they have played out many, many times. The only question for you is whether you step into their 'game' and allow them to make you the 'teacher', or whether you choose to set your own rules by taking control at the start.

Essentially, you are caught up in their preconceptions of anyone who dares to stand at the front of one of their meeting rooms. Once you enter the room, other preconceptions get added into the mix too.

All of these disruptive behaviours are designed to get attention. Unfortunately, in order for you to get your message across, you need the audience's attention. Any member of the audience who competes for attention will prevent you from achieving your outcome.

I know that it can be uncomfortable to deal with these disruptions, so I don't blame you if you avoid the potential conflict because I have done it myself. And as a direct result, I lost control of the pitch and lost the business. What happens in your pitch is entirely up to you. The only crime is not learning from your mistakes.

Another thing to bear in mind is that one person will not stay in a single role; they will respond to other people and their behaviour.

For example, someone may begin as the teacher's pet, giving you lots of approving feedback and asking encouraging questions. If they don't get what they want, namely control of the situation, they can switch roles and become the class supervisor. Because they know that their colleague won't stand for their superior posturing, their attempts to tell other people what to do are rejected so they sulk, then they start whispering to their colleagues, then they start asking awkward questions to draw you into a conversation. You end up wasting a significant amount of your pitch trying to control someone who you failed to control in the first place because they seemed nice.

Feedback from the audience is all very well, but if it doesn't help you to get your message across, it's disruptive. Take control.

Making an Impression

Back in Secret Three, we looked at the different communication channels that we use to broadcast our intentions, and we've also talked about setting out your territory when you enter the room.

When you walk into the room, the audience will make their minds up about you in two to three seconds. In one glance, they will assess your credibility, social status, emotional state and intentions.

The non-verbal information that you radiate will lay the foundation for everything that happens from the moment you enter the room. We have also talked about the concept of mental rehearsal, and how you can prepare yourself for the pitch in the way that professional athletes prepare for a race.

Putting all of these elements together means that you can be aware of the impression that you want to create and you can be objective in recognising anything that is going to hinder you.

You are broadcasting information on all channels whether you like it or not, so make sure that you have a clear and realistic outcome in mind and that you understand exactly why you are pitching.

When you enter the room, you must claim your territory. That does not mean that you walk in like you own the place, because that actually sends the signal that you don't belong there. Walk in like you walk into your own home, and if anything is not to your liking, change it. This is your unique opportunity to pitch, so why wouldn't you want everything to be perfect?

91% of employers[4] equate an applicant's dress and grooming with their attitude towards their potential employer. 95% equate the applicant's suitability for the job with their appearance.

A global household name in the Internet market employs sales people who go and pitch their services to corporate clients. When I was helping them to develop their pitching skills, I noticed that they turned up to pitch to clients wearing torn T shirts and jeans. They said that this was part of the image they want to create, that the

---

4 Jobweb.com annual survey, 2002

client should look past their preconceptions and see the value of their innovative products and services.

They said that their clients expect to see them unshaven, wearing their gardening clothes. They said, "We're that kind of company. That's our image." and they were very defensive about it.

An artist can argue until he's blue in the face that his work communicates an important message, but if the customer doesn't like it, he doesn't buy it. Beauty is indeed in the eye of the beholder.

While art should, of course, have cultural merit that transcends its commercial value, most artists do like to eat occasionally, and so the successful ones quickly learn one of two approaches to marketing. They either paint what their customers want, regardless of whether they think it's any good or not, or they paint what they want and look for the potential customers who like it. The more people don't like it, the more their work will be appreciated by the people who do like it. They polarise opinion and, in doing so, create a stronger brand and more customer loyalty.

However, that isn't what was happening at this company. The reality was that their potential customers weren't taking them seriously.

There's a trend in marketing that we could call 'anti-branding'. It includes plain packaging, social media marketing and radical brand names such as "Water" for bottled water.

Dressing like a tramp is not anti-branding, although it certainly is memorable. While they say that 'no publicity is bad publicity', it depends on what you want to be remembered for. You also have to remember that you're not pitching to be a celebrity, you're pitching for business. The criteria for appearing in a tabloid newspaper are quite different to the criteria for making a business investment.

A senior manager at the company told me of his dissatisfaction with the sales people, saying that their approach is to, "show up and throw up". In other words, they turn up at a client's offices dressed like they've just gotten out of bed on a Sunday morning and then throw data at the audience as if that was going to be enough. A lot of charts, data and raw, meaningless technical information.

An old adage in sales training is, "telling is not selling".

One way of looking at it is that the sales people don't believe that they are taken seriously at a corporate level, so rather than try to compete by wearing suits and ties, they go the opposite way, as if they're teenagers rebelling against their parents. They're presenting the client with a challenge; "Respect me because of my knowledge, in spite of your preconceptions". Unfortunately, they're not teenagers and the clients are not their parents, and the result is that the client is distinctly unimpressed.

When the client decides they don't want to do business with the kind of person who doesn't bother shaving or getting dressed for a business meeting, it's no use blaming them. It's no use saying that the client is short sighted because they couldn't see beyond your image, and after all, that is your company's image. It's the way you are. Take it or leave it. Because, equally, the client can say, "Here are the people we like to do business with. These are the people we trust to support our business. These are the people we feel we can rely on. These are the people we spend our money with. Take it or leave it."

The sales people at this Internet company said, "Well if a client's going to be like that, I don't want to do business with them". Right. So if the client won't let you act like a teenager, you don't want to do business with them anyway. How mature.

I'm not saying that you always have to wear a suit, I'm saying that you have to remove your appearance as a potential barrier between you and the audience.

This could equally work the other way, because rapport is a sign that two or more people feel they are somehow alike. If you pitched to this Internet company in your best pinstripe suit, bowler hat and silk tie, they might equally feel that you were too 'stuffy' for them, too 'traditional', too 'inflexible'.

What we're talking about is a culture clash. Clothes are part of what marks out our social status and affiliation, and we communicate that affiliation when meeting a new client for the first time. If you're both in suits, fine. If you're both in jeans, fine. Although I might still argue that scruffy T shirts and jeans are not generally the mark of someone who is serious about his or her business.

The mismatch, the misalignment comes when one person is dressed so differently to another that they might as well be wearing different street gang insignia.

The way you look is important, not because I say so but because your potential client will draw a conclusion from it, and on that conclusion, they will base their decision to buy from you.

3.8 First Impressions

Have you ever made up your mind about someone just from the way that they looked?

Why?

Do you think people have done the same to you?

Has that always worked in your favour?

Why would you limit the number of people who you can sell to, simply because of what you're wearing?

Your appearance communicates with your audience long before you open your mouth, so make sure you're saying what you intend to say.

Non-Verbal Communication

The first and most important thing about rapport is to be in rapport with yourself. Self doubt and confusion lead to incongruence that other people will pick up on instantly.

Incongruence is a state of misalignment between something and its context. For example, an elephant on ice skates is incongruous. A double glazing sales person saying, "I'm just going to go outside for a moment and pretend to phone my manager for a discount, but really we'll be talking about football" is incongruous.

Incongruity is a fish out of water. As with almost everything else we're discussing, it's all about perception. Incongruity is not what you expect, so it seems odd, it stands out and it feels out of place. You walk into your house and instantly know that something has been moved. You look at the face of someone you love and you know something is wrong.

We learn that everything has a context, and we know instantly when that balance is disturbed.

In this situation, we're discussing incongruity in the specific context of language – both verbal and non-verbal.

The non-verbal elements of language place the verbal elements in their proper context, because words alone are vague and ambiguous.

I'm sure you've had the experience of not hearing someone quite right, with either amusing, confusing or insulting results.

Hypnotherapists use this ambiguity in a constructive way, as tonal ambiguity leads to confusion at the unconscious level which in turn can lead to a 'hypnotic trance'. Some people also call this 'phonological ambiguity'; the effect of two words which sound the same but do not have the same meaning. It's like trying to make sense of two conflicting messages at the same time.

How would you feel if you asked someone a question and they said both 'yes' and 'no' at the same time? Of course, a person can't say both words at once, so they say 'yes' with their voice and 'no' with a shake of their head and a shaky voice tone.

Your hear 'yes' but you know they're really not sure about it.

In 1969, the social psychologist Albert Mehrabian and his assistant Argyle performed a study which is probably the best known work ever carried out on communication and influence.

Mehrabian and Argyle gave subjects words and phrases to read to each other and paired those words with different intonations and facial expressions. What they deduced from this was that the overall meaning that we take from a message is a combination of factors; some verbal and some non-verbal.

The verbal components of language are simply the words and their underlying structure of grammar and syntax.

The non-verbal components include voice tone, volume, pitch, intonation as well as facial expressions and body movements.

The result of Mehrabian and Argyle's work is this famous pie chart:

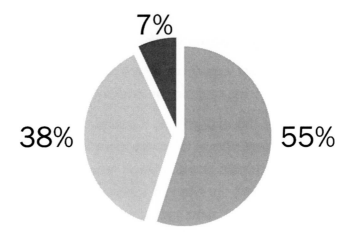

Visual Non-Verbal	Tonal Non-Verbal	Verbal
55%	38%	7%
Facial expressions	Pitch	Words
Hands	Volume	
Body	Intonation	
	Pace	
	Rhythm	

Not everyone agrees with these figures, and some people even dispute the original research. I just want to make it clear that words are not the only form of communication between human beings. If you don't agree, then just ask yourself if you have ever been misunderstood, or if you have ever picked up on an unspoken signal from someone, or if you have ever been blind to someone's sarcasm or sincerity because of your own point of view.

If you want to check the figures for yourself, it's always best to conduct your own, independent research. Here's how.

3.9 Non-Verbal Communication

You'll need a group of people for this, perhaps ten or more. Your next team meeting might be an ideal time to try this, or get a group of colleagues together in a quiet meeting room. It also works best if the presenter is someone who the rest of the group has not seen presenting recently.

Ask someone to present for 20 seconds on a subject of their choosing. Ask the group to write down the first five things that they notice.

When the 20 seconds has elapsed, stop the presenter and ask everyone to count their observations.

Make a note of the number of:

Things they saw

Things they heard, as in specific words

Things they heard, as in voice tone, pauses, accent, ums and ahs etc.

Total everyone's figures up and work them out as a percentage of the total.

Let's say that your numbers are 78 'saw', 62 'tone' and 9 'heard'. Add them all together, that's 149. Now divide each one into the total, so that's 78/149 = 0.52 for 'saw'. That's 52% of the overall communication.

In this example, 'tone' is 42% and 'words' are 6%.

If you want to draw a pie chart, just multiply your results by 12 and draw imaginary hands on a clock face. That puts 'saw' at about half past six, 'words' at just past eleven o'clock and 'tone' is the space in between. Easy!

In all the dozens of times I've done this experiment during training courses, these figures are very typical. The only thing that really affects the 'words' figure is when the presenter is speaking about a subject that is very relevant to the group, for example on a very hot day when the presenter was talking about ice cold beer. Everyone heard the words "cold beer"!

For our purposes, incongruence occurs when a speaker exhibits a conflict between any or all of these three components of communication. For example, with a smile on their face, your boss tells you that they're sorry but they've got to let you go. Or, with wide eyes and shaking hands, your partner tells you that they're fine.

You know that there's something missing, you just don't know what.

Aside from a simple nod or shake of the head, the non-verbal components of communication provide the context within which we make sense of the verbal component. The overall message is therefore a combination of the two.

When your audience detects incongruity, people may not recognise it consciously but they will still find it hard to accept what you say. When you're in an incongruent state, you're more likely to generate confusion and doubt in other people. You may choose to do this, in which case incongruence is a very useful tool.

3.10 Getting the Message

If you're at a presentation in the near future, take a few minutes to observe every single part of the speaker that communicates part of his or her overall message. Observe their eyes, eyebrows, hands, fingers, shoulders, legs, feet, breathing, mouth, cheeks, head, everything that you can.

Make a list of each component and, looking at it in isolation, work out what message they are conveying and if their communication is congruent.

If you don't have a presentation to attend, watch the unscripted interviews on an extended news and current affairs TV program.

An imbalance in your own thoughts and intentions is communicated over multiple channels, all of which are received and processed by your audience. The result is that they feel the same unease, the same conflict, and they attribute that to you. Rapport turns out to be a double edged sword. Without it, you communicate nothing. With it, you communicate everything, whether you intend to or not. You can't hide anything when you're in rapport.

What is actually happening is that there is not one single communication channel between two people, or between one person and an audience. Every part of your body that can convey information does convey information, constantly.

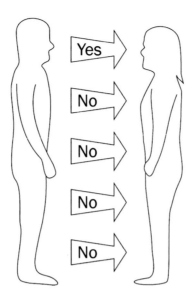

It's entirely possible to communicate multiple messages at the same time, using these different channels. I'm not saying that you should try to do this consciously, I'm merely pointing out that you will not be aware of many of the ways in which you're broadcasting your true thoughts, feelings and intentions.

Don't try to force or contrive your body language. Non-verbal communication is far too complex to make it up as you go along, which is why it's so valuable for you to observe in other people.

When your words, voice, eyes, hands and body all communicate the same information, your message is reinforced and your audience will receive it, loud and clear. You could say that you're speaking from your head and heart at the same time, and no-one can fake that.

Eye Movements

Now that we have explored the principles of non-verbal communication, we can spend some time observing the audience.

At first, it's not easy to pitch and observe at the same time, which is one reason why it's so valuable to pitch as a team. One of the team can focus entirely on the pitch, another can observe the audience.

Observing and interpreting non-verbal communication is the subject of an entire book in itself, so I'm going to cover just some of the aspects that are most practical for considering when you're pitching, one of which is eye movement.

I'm not talking about broad facial expressions such as surprise or "oh no, not again" which can be signalled with expressions that centre around the eyes. I'm talking about the way that our eye movements reveal our inner thought processes.

Whilst some research has been done in this area, it is greatly debated. It seems that the more specific meaning that we attach to eye movements, or 'body language', or dreams, the more debate that creates. In any case, the generalisations are useful to us because they're easy to remember, practical and observable, most of the time.

Aardman Animations, the creators of Wallace and Grommit, have eye movements down to a fine art. Watch any of their animations and take time to notice the way that characters move their eyes.

People hardly ever stop thinking. They're thinking while they're talking, while you're talking, while they're thinking about talking, even while they're talking about thinking.

Our thoughts are a constant stream of information, some external and some internal. When we are processing internal information, we could call that 'thinking', and when we think, we use the same parts of our brain as we use for taking in new, external information.

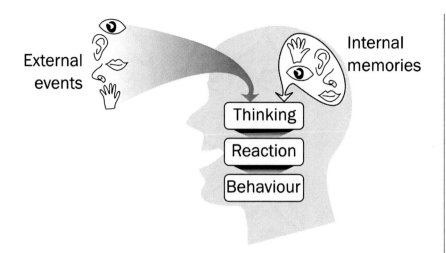

External events

Internal memories

Thinking

Reaction

Behaviour

The way that we know this is that scientists have put people into brain scanners that show which part of the brain the person is using for a particular task. Increased blood flow infers increased activity and the latest 'functional MRI' (Magnetic Resonance Imaging) scanners can produce videos of the brain working in real time.

When a person takes in new information, the parts of their brain that process external senses activates, then a few milliseconds later, the part that makes sense of this and creates a reaction fires up.

When the same person imagines the same information, their initial sensory areas don't activate, but everything else does, as if the brain treats both internal and external information equally.

So what we have established is that we think using our senses, and since every memory, thought and experience we have ever had can be broken down into an image, sound, feeling taste or smell, we have a very useful way to tap into someone's imagination or understand how they think.

Secret 3: Steady, Ready, Pitch

Seeing

Hearing

Feeling

Pitch blindness
from looking at
too many slides
in a darkened
room

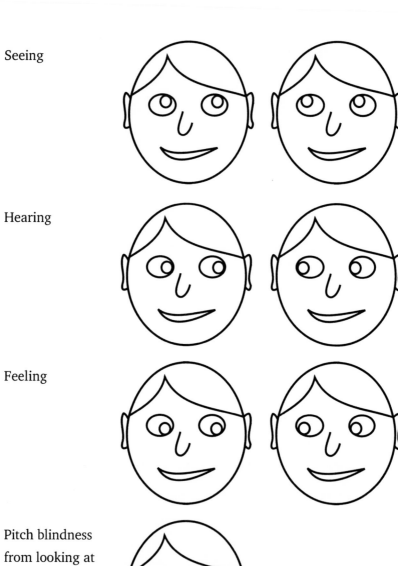

3.11 Eye Movement

Find a willing friend or colleague to help you with this exercise.

Memorise each question and then look the person right in the eye as you ask it. If you read from the page, you will miss the eye movement as it will happen as soon as the person understands the question - which is long before you have finished reading it.

What colour is your bedroom ceiling?

Where is the bed in relation to the window?

What would your bedroom look like if it were a different colour?

When you pull back the curtains, what sound do they make?

What sound would they make if you pulled them faster?

What sound would they make if you pulled them back slower?

What do they feel like?

How easily do the curtains move?

What can you feel with your toes?

How do you feel when you hear chalk used on a blackboard?

How does your favourite person's voice make you feel?

Say to yourself inside your head, "Mary had a little lamb"

Say to yourself inside your head, using the voice of a cartoon character, "Mary had a little lamb"

What's the thing you enjoy doing most?

You will probably notice your subject's eyes moving about rather than going to one place and staying there. This is an example of something known as a 'pattern'. For example, if you asked the question, "How easily do the curtains move?", they may look up to the left, then up to the right, then down to the right before answering. This indicates them trying to see their curtains move, then making up a picture of their curtains, then finally checking the image against the feelings in their muscles. You can check your interpretation with them after they answer the question.

Observing someone's eye movements when you ask them a question gives you an insight into how they are organising their thoughts, and that in turn tells you how best to communicate with them, which is something we'll be exploring in detail in Secret Five.

Credibility

Can you believe that we're almost at the point where you're going to open your mouth and say your first words?

Can you guess what they might be?

We are a social species, and one of the things that we do very well is to communicate with each other. We've talked about the importance of non-verbal communication, and one of the things that we need to ascertain about any stranger is their intentions. If a stranger approaches, do they want to join your herd and share your resources, or are they are predator?

The first question that will be on the audience's mind is:

"Who are you and what do you want?"

The answer to that question is where you gain credibility.

You may have heard of the idea of an 'elevator pitch' which is a condensed version of your pitch, lasting perhaps as little as 30 seconds. Some people try to cram as much information as possible into their 30 seconds but this is not helpful and can actually damage your credibility.

We'll come on to elevator pitches in a moment, but I've mentioned them now because of the way that they heighten the need to answer the client's initial questions before they can hear your pitch. If you launch right into your pitch, it's like talking before the other person has even picked the phone up.

In addition to, "Who are you and what do you want?", the audience will have other questions as you begin your pitch. They will almost never say these questions out loud, but they will be there in the background and until these questions are answered, the audience cannot give you their full attention.

The audience's unspoken questions can include:

☐ Do we have anything in common?

☐ Do I like you?

☐ Do I believe you?

☐ Do I trust you?

☐ Do you believe yourself?

☐ Do you know what you're talking about?

☐ Is this relevant to me?

☐ Do I respect you?

The more these questions are answered by your pitch, the more the audience can hear what you're saying.

If you launch into the pitch too early, trying to cram in as many words as possible, you run a significant risk that the client will stare blankly at you, wondering, "Why are you telling me this?" And while those questions are running around in the client's head, they are not listening to a word you're saying, or at least they're not listening in the way that you would want them to.

A little bit of intrigue and curiosity at the start of your pitch isn't a bad thing, but make sure it's just enough to hook the client and not enough to confuse them.

Consistency

Traditional presentation training advocated an 'ice breaker' approach. This presumes that there is some ice to break, an initial uncomfortable silence. Many presenters still start with a joke or informal comment. In a pitch this can be dangerous.

For your pitch to have its maximum impact, it must be consistent. No personal small talk. No comparison of golf handicaps or football results. No enquiries about the wife, weekend or future holiday plans.

By all means, make small talk. Just make it relevant. There is so much happening in your client's business that there is plenty to talk about prior to the actual pitch. Read the news on their website. Read about their competitors. Keep them on track. Let them know that they are there to talk business, not for a free slide show and afternoon tea.

As an extra bonus, while your colleague is setting up the laptop and other paraphernalia, you have the audience's undivided attention at perhaps the most critical time during the whole pitch – the time during which the audience aren't being critical, because they don't know that the pitch has already started.

How many pitches have you sat through or delivered where the presenter made small talk while his or her colleague was getting the presentation ready?

Worse still, have you ever seen the presenter ignore the audience completely while he or she plays with the slides, making last minute changes. I remember walking into a meeting room to see the presenter making last minute changes to his slide set. Without looking up, he said, "I'll be with you in a minute", and in those seven words, he told me that the most important part of the pitch wasn't the audience, or even his message. The most important thing to him was the running order of his slides. He had to work a great deal harder to get my attention after that.

Compare these two examples of how you might use this 'set up time'.

"It will just take Fred a few minutes to set up before we get started. So, how was your weekend? Did you see the match? Oh, they're going to struggle this season, aren't they? Oh right we're all set. OK then. Ladies and gentlemen, I'd like to take this opportunity to..."

"Just as we're setting up for our pitch to you today, I want to make sure we're going to cover everything you need to make an informed decision today, and also I'd like to check exactly how much time we have your undivided attention for, because I do appreciate you're busy and your schedules can change at short notice.... (waits for answer) so in that case for the next 30 minutes I would like to take this opportunity to..."

Do you see the difference?

Do you see how this relates to a trailer for a film?

If you think for a moment about rapport, one of the important things that happens during the first few minutes of being in the room is that the audience forms an initial impression of you and puts you in a box.

Let's say you have a local greengrocer's shop, just round the corner. You go there two or three times a week and he always has fresh fruit and vegetables, and a few tips on recipes for you. Everything is so fresh, you just love picking up something new that you haven't tried before. One day, you call in to find that he's started up an Internet cafe in the corner of the shop. Does it make any sense to you? Do you find yourself thinking, "No! He's my greengrocer, not a dot com Millionaire!" Whether it's a good idea or not, most people don't like it because it's different.

Food and drinks manufacturers tinker with our favourite recipes. Whether their focus groups think they're better or not in a blind taste test, we don't like them. The only reason that we don't like them is that they're not what we have become accustomed to.

We like familiarity, in fact we crave it. We like things to be the way that we think they are. If that nice man who talks about football and what I did at the weekend starts talking to me about business, I don't like it one bit. That's not what he's there for. He's there to chat, not to sell.

Filling gaps with social chit-chat breaks rapport. Some sales people, having established rapport in the context of sport or hobbies, find it so hard to break that rapport that they spend the entire meeting making small talk. Everybody goes away wondering what that was all about.

From the very moment that you first make contact with the client on pitch day, let them know that you mean business. Yes, you're a nice, sociable person. Yes, you are easy to get along with. But the only basis for your relationship at that time is business. You don't need to know about their hobbies because you won't be visiting the philatelist with them. You don't need to know about their children because you won't be going to the park with them. You only need to know about their business and what they want to achieve, professionally. This does not negate being sociable and knowing about their personal lives at other more appropriate times.

Therefore, your opening has to both grab the audience's attention and fit seamlessly with the overall message and direction of your pitch.

Opening

Finally, it's time for your big opening. By paying attention so far, you have learned the essential principles of the pitch and you have created your outline, format and content.

Over the next two Secrets, we'll be exploring the delivery of the main part of your pitch content.

Opening your pitch means much more than simply beginning speaking. It takes much more than a simple, "Good morning, my name is Fred and I'm here to tell you about..." to create a firm foundation for your entire pitch.

Signposting

What I'm going to be telling you about is...

The best known example of signposting is probably the old adage of "tell them what you're going to tell them, tell them and then tell them what you've told them".

You might briefly explain:

- ☐ Who you are
- ☐ Why are you pitching
- ☐ What's in it for the audience
- ☐ What you're going to talk about
- ☐ When the audience can ask questions
- ☐ Anything else you're going to include in your pitch

The Outcome

By the end of this pitch...

If you state your outcome to the audience, everyone is clear about why they are there. If you think back to the outcome exercise in Secret Two, you may recall that an outcome must be under your control. Therefore, if you tell the audience that, by the end of your pitch, they will decide to buy your product, your outcome is not under your control and you'll probably irritate the audience too.

People generally don't like being told what to do, especially if they think they're in charge.

A better outcome would be that the audience will reach a conclusion, because that is quite likely to happen anyway. Without your pitch, they would reach that conclusion in the absence of any information from you that might influence their conclusion. You can't control their decision, but you do hope to influence it.

You might say, "Based on my proposal, you may already have a decision in mind. Whether that's the case or not, my aim today is to give you the information you need to make a decision. I'll be direct and say that I'd like you to choose to work with me. I respect that it's entirely your decision to make, so my job is to give you what you need to reach what I hope will be a favourable decision."

There's no harm in saying that you want the client's business. It's all too easy to assume that everyone knows it and instead act as if your role is to inform or educate the client. It's not.

Sometimes, sales people introduce themselves as area managers, or consultants, or specialists, or account directors. If you have a vested interest in the client buying from you then you are a sales person. The client knows it, regardless of your job title.

By stating your outcome, you clearly imply your role and that lets the audience know the context within which you are building rapport, and that in turn makes it easier for you to gain rapport and develop the right working relationship.

One Word

Pitching. That's what it's all about.

If a word sums up your entire pitch, or the problem that your proposal solves, then you can start with that word. Leave it hanging in the air for a moment before you continue, so that you don't lose its impact.

The Contradiction

It was the best of times, it was the worst of times.

Some of our customer say that ours is the best product they've ever used. I disagree.

Many people have told me that this is the best book on the art of pitching that they have ever read. I'm not so sure.

We all know that vitamins are good for us. But I'm going to show you that it's not always true.

The contradiction begins with something familiar and turns it on its head, creating curiosity and sometimes encouraging the audience to side 'against' the presenter and therefore 'with' the pitch itself.

The Quotation

"It was the best of times, it was the worst of times"

"Henry Ford said that 'if there is any one secret of success, it lies in the ability to get the other person's point of view and see things from that person's angle as well as your own'. In preparation for our pitch today, we've spent some time with your people so that we can see things from your angle."

"Charles Schwab said that when you put a limit on what you will do, you put a limit on what you can do. Today, I'm asking you to suspend your beliefs for just fifteen minutes and think not about what you have done in the past but what you can do, about what is possible."

"E. Joseph Crossman said that 'obstacles are things a person sees when he takes his eyes off his goal'. I've certainly overcome my fair share of obstacles in getting to where I am today, and I have never taken my eyes off my goal of getting the support I need to make my business a great success."

"Louis Pasteur's work has saved countless lives, but he also suffered from ridicule from the established scientific community when he first announced his discoveries. Some people will always ridicule what's new, what they don't understand, yet intelligent, open minded people welcome new ideas that challenge established routines. Louis Pasteur himself said that 'chance favours the prepared mind' and so I'm asking you today to be prepared for the chance, the opportunity to experience something new and make an open, unbiased decision."

The Dramatic Entrance

If you open your pitch with dramatic impact, you might certainly get the audience's attention, although you potentially create a high energy opening which you then have to work harder to maintain.

You can combine the principle of this opening with the Show and Tell, for example using an object which you can break at some point during the pitch to make a point.

For example, you could relate the concept of hidden value to the idea of an antique vase that has been in your garage for years until you saw the same vase on television. You could use the vase as a metaphor for having something that you don't appreciate the true value of. At the end of your pitch, to make a point about wasting an opportunity, you could drop the vase and smash it. Of course, the vase is actually worthless, but the impact on the audience will be very real.

Imagine

Invite the audience to imagine themselves in a situation; either new or familiar.

"Imagine your first day at school..."

"Imagine a world where..."

Inviting the audience to imagine will tend to draw them into a more relaxed, receptive frame of mind. Just be sure to bring their attention firmly back to the room before you continue with your pitch.

Humour

If you want to introduce your pitch with humour, start easy. Use personal experiences, oddities, irony. The more personal, the more universal. Let the audience laugh at you, not at themselves.

Avoid telling jokes unless you're selling your services as a stand up comedian. This has nothing to do with your ability to tell jokes, it is because telling jokes and then moving into a business pitch breaks rapport. By opening with a joke, you establish your role as that of entertainer, not as business partner.

There is a place for levity and lightness but the best pitchers simply allow humour to flow from the situation if and when it is appropriate.

The Reference

If the company you're pitching to has a current, relevant news story or event, you can open your pitch with a reference to it.

The Promise

At the beginning of your pitch, make a prediction or promise. You can combine this with the previous tip by placing an answer in an envelope or box.

For example, you might promise that by the end of the pitch, a million births and deaths will have taken place in the room. In the box is a glass plate with bacteria on, to show the audience the power of your disinfectant product.

Show and Tell

You can use any object as a metaphor for the main message of your pitch. It might be something that literally represents your pitch, such as a product of demonstration model, or it might be a metaphor for the message of your pitch.

With this format, you can revisit your object throughout your pitch and use it in your closing too. It might even be something that you can leave at the front of the room when you leave, to serve as a reminder.

The Question

Instead of starting your pitch with a grand opening statement, why not start with a question?

Imagine you're at a conference. You meet with someone who you would dearly love to do business with.

You say, "What one thing could we show you today that would make the whole conference worthwhile?"

Whatever they say, that's what you talk about. The entire pitch, centred around the one idea that will make the biggest difference to them.

A question gets the listener's attention like nothing else. You can stand on a street corner, shouting all day and before long, your pitch will become background noise. But ask someone a question and, even for a moment, they are hooked. They are instantly put into a receptive frame of mind. After that, it's up to you to put their attention to good use.

We're going to explore the use of questions in much more detail in Secret Five, Mind Your Language. How much are you looking forward to it?

Closing the Loop

Many stories and films end with the same words as they open with. In children's fiction, The Gruffalo(which, when my son Sam was younger, I must have read with him over a hundred times) ends with the same two lines as it opens with. The film Forrest Gump starts and ends with a very similar scene, showing a white feather floating in the breeze. This looping neatly concludes a story and wraps everything together.

You could open your pitch with a powerful statement, such as a compelling statistic or a call to action and then repeat that statement as you conclude your pitch.

Starting and ending with the same question is very powerful when your question is a thought provoking one.

Here are some examples with the subject of their pitch:

Question	Subject
"What would you give to be able to correct one mistake in your life?"	A project to support disadvantaged teenagers
"How would you feel if you could save one more life today?"	Funding for a health program
"What would you do with an extra £10,000 in your business budget?"	An IT project that would lead to a cost saving of £10,000
"What would it take for you to make the right decision today?"	A general purpose question for any pitch that invites a decision
"How would you feel, knowing that you had changed the world today?"	Investment in a product that will save energy, cure an illness or markedly improve people's lives
"What makes the difference between a good advert and a great advert?"	An advertising campaign
"What would it mean to you to hear your name spoken in every house in the country"	An advertising campaign

The idea is very simple. Begin by posing the question. After leaving it to hang in the air for a few moments, move straight into your pitch. Do not obviously refer back to your opening question. At the end of your pitch, repeat the question. The content of your pitch has provided the answer, and the audience now knows what to do.

Here's an example script.

"What would you give to be able to correct one mistake in your life?

My name is Stevie Smith and I run a project for teenagers who have been in trouble with the police. Typically, they struggled at school, dropped out and got into the wrong company. Through peer pressure, which I know we've all felt in one way or another, they end up making a mistake that they regret for the rest of their lives. Through our project, that I'm seeking your support with, we help these teenagers to put right that mistake and to make sure it doesn't take away their chance of a normal life, the kind of life that it's easy for people like us to take for granted.

I'm asking for your sponsorship, your time, your brand or just your funding. Which you give is up to you, all are invaluable to us and to the teenagers who are going to benefit so much from your help.

After all, what would you give to be able to correct one mistake in your life?"

You'll probably notice that this script incorporates a few other elements that we've been discussing too. It builds rapport with a universal truth (peer pressure), it tells a story, it adds more rapport (people like us), it has a call to action, it presupposes that the audience will give at least one form of support, it shows gratitude, and it presupposes that the audience has already decided to help. Even the question itself puts the audience into the place of these disadvantaged teenagers, creating an emotional link that is very hard to turn away from, especially for anyone who has ever felt disadvantaged themselves, or for anyone who has ever been given a second chance in life. The question takes on a different meaning as a result of what you say in the main body of the pitch, because the second question is now set in the context of greater empathy.

The Old Curiosity Shop

Before you begin your pitch, place a mysterious object in plain sight of the audience. It might be a cardboard box, an envelope, an ornament, a toy or a picture. It can be anything that in some way relates to the message that you want to get across.

For example. let's say you're pitching a business idea for a water saving device, so you place three bags of sugar on the lectern or table. At the end of your pitch, you illustrate the value of water by pointing out that every member of the audience's body is between 97% and 99% water, so if you took all of the water out of a human body, the sugar is the weight of what would remain. You can end by saying that we have to save water because, without water, this is all that is left of us.

If you have used a plain cardboard box, you can pull out pretty much anything you like to emphasise your point.

The Surprise

Write some information such as numbers on the whiteboard. At the right point in your pitch, tell the audience what the numbers mean.

For example, let's say that you write the following during a pitch about a new product that helps children to learn to read.

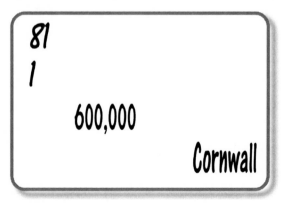

When you reach the relevant moments in your pitch, you can fill in the missing clues, either all at once or step by step as you build your pitch:

81% of the world's population is literate

1% of the UK's population cannot read & write

That's 600,000 people in the UK!

The entire population of Cornwall

You can also see from this example that raw statistics are not very compelling. They're just numbers, and when you translate those numbers into something that the audience can relate to emotionally, your pitch takes on a whole new level of impact.

The Story

When people first started to ask when I was ever going to write a book, I thought that I would never find the time. Over the years, though, I gradually started recording some of my experiences, and before I knew it, I had the basis of the Seven Secrets. Since then, I made a concerted effort to form those Seven Secrets into something more tangible, and the result is in your hands, right now.

You can open your pitch with a story. It might be a well known story, a children's story, a story from your distant past or even a story about your journey to the client's offices.

Here's What I Want You To Do

What does a magician do? He tells the audience exactly what he is doing. What happens when he then tells the audience what to do? They generally do it.

Some 'Vegas' style magicians don't speak but instead instruct the audience using mysterious, exaggerated movements and expressions.

Modern magicians tend not to do this as they think it's a bit clichéd, so instead they do exactly the same but in a more subtle way. They know that the result is vital, regardless of how they achieve it.

For example, the magician picks up a coin in his left hand. He doesn't need to point at it. He doesn't need to say, "ladies and gentlemen, observe that the coin is now in my left hand". He doesn't need to raise his eyebrows and look obviously at his left hand. The more he draws attention to it, the more he makes the audience question it. In fact, the magician wants the audience to almost forget the coin is there, because it isn't really there anyway. The magician instructs the audience by implication.

In a pitch, it is a good idea to get the audience following instructions. You are there for your benefit, not as a servant of the client. You are entering into a mutually beneficial, equal business partnership. You are not anyone's slave, nor master. Having said that, while you're pitching, you are in control of the room. Think of your role as being like a nominated fire officer at work. You're not in charge, you're no more or less important than anyone else, but in certain situations, everyone knows that it's in their best interests to follow your lead.

One of the aspects of good sales practice is to take the lead in the relationship from an early stage by asking the client to do things for you; provide information or arrange a meeting room, for example. In the pitch, you can ask the client to arrange the room a certain way, provide some water, even pass you a pen.

Getting the client into the habit of doing things that you ask is very important in defining your relationship with them. The alternative is that you do everything they ask, ask them for nothing in return and when you ask for an order, they ask you for more discounts, more concessions and more time, because they have trained you to respond to them. At the very least, the playing field needs to be level.

Timing

The bigger the risk of the opening, the more important your timing.

Drama, a joke, suspense all rely on timing, and timing is the thing that will suffer if you feel nervous.

If you feel any nerves or anxiety at all, go for a soft opening such as a story. This allows you to relax into your pitch before you reach the pause and give your audience time to reflect on the story before moving into the main body of your pitch.

If you're nervous and your focus is on yourself, your sense of time will change. You might feel that you have been talking for a long time, only to find that you've rushed through your pitch in just five minutes. When you get drawn into a conversation, or if you're asked a difficult question, what seems like a few seconds to you can be minutes for the audience.

Pausing is an important way to add impact to your pitch. As a simple rule of thumb, a pause should be just long enough that you think it's too long.

If you feel that timing is an issue, remember a very simple tip. Keep an eye on the clock.

Never, Never, Ever

Apologise

For the start, the food, the weather, the confusion, the length of your pitch, the boredom, the time of day, for wasting the audience's time, for being alive.

Make a Bad Joke

Never make a joke at the expense of someone in the audience, even if you think you know them really well and they're all like mates really and you're always joking around. It's unprofessional and it alienates you. Keep jokes like this for the pub.

Try to build rapport by saying you're like the audience. You're not like them, otherwise you would be sitting where they are.

Make the Audience Wait

Remember the presenter who was busy making changes to his slides as the audience entered the room. Without looking up he said, "I'll be with you in a minute".

Accidents do happen. Last minute power cuts, for example, do occur and they do cause problems.

I've waited countless times while presenters explained how it all worked fine this morning, or they can't understand why it isn't working, or that it really should work. The audience has a little patience, but beyond that, they really do expect a presenter to be better prepared.

Another simple rule of thumb applies here – never go into a pitch, relying on something that you cannot pitch without.

Computer slides might reinforce your pitch but they are not your pitch. Product samples and demonstrations need to work right, first time. Videos need to play smoothly. Internet connections need to be working, and working fast.

If you're in any doubt, do without.

Stick to the Script

When you understand your pitch inside out, you can adapt easily to work around any technical problems.

If you think back to the pitch design format in Secret Two, you may recall that the last step is 'practice'. When you practice your pitch, you know exactly what you are aiming for, and you can achieve that in many ways.

If your computer crashes, you can seamlessly sketch something on the whiteboard. If your product demonstration doesn't work, you can move onto a story that illustrates the product in use.

The audience doesn't expect your pitch to be perfect. Very few clients want to buy something 'off the shelf', so if something isn't quite right, it's an opportunity for the client to be involved in its development. If the design or format isn't quite what the client had in mind, you have the opportunity to shape your pitch around what they do have in mind, or at least to discuss the differences.

Being able to adapt does not mean that you make it up as you go along. Believing that you can present 'off the cuff' is a sign of poor preparation, and that is a bad thing.

Winston Churchill said that he spent the best years of his life preparing for his impromptu speeches.

Some presenters use small cards to remind themselves of their key points. There's no problem with doing this, although I would advise that you write as few words as possible on a card so that you don't have to spend time reading them, and you should number the cards in case they get mixed up.

An alternative is to draw a picture or icon on each card, as you may find you can take this in much more quickly and without interrupting the flow of your pitch.

Follow Advice

You'll be plagued with friends and colleagues offering you good advice about your pitch. Do this, don't do that. Don't listen to what works for someone else, because that's what works for them. Keep on working at what works for you.

Secret Brief

Making a Connection

Make sure you have the audience's full attention before you say a word.

State

Your state shapes how you feel, how you perceive and how you behave.

Anchoring

Anchoring is a powerful method for accessing the state you want, and you can influence the audience's state too. On top of that, it's natural, organic and has zero calories.

Rapport

A connection between two or more people, an invisible communication medium and a powerful means of influence.

Group Rapport

The audience will act as a single entity, so make sure you're in control.

I'm Sorry, I'm Losing You

What do you do if you lose rapport? You need to decide before you pitch, not hope for the best and work it out as you go along.

Influence

Rapport is a two way street, so don't be so preoccupied with influencing the audience that you don't notice how much they're influencing you.

Territory

A good pitcher claims his or her territory and controls it for the duration of the pitch.

Making an Impression

The audience forms an impression of you in two to three seconds, and you have a high degree of control over that impression.

Non-Verbal Communication

Whilst some people debate the relative impact of verbal and non-verbal communication, we can at least agree that human beings communicate over multiple channels, and have very little conscious control over that process. Therefore, your true intentions leak out and in return, your audience broadcasts their reaction back to you.

Credibility

Before the audience can properly pay attention and put what you say into its proper context, you need to establish your credibility. This will happen whether you like it or not, so it's best to take control and make the right impression.

Interruptions

Once you have decided how you want to handle interruptions, stick to it. If you want to let the audience take control of your pitch, you do more harm by making a half hearted effort. To be in control you have to risk being firm.

Consistency

Keeping the content and direction of your pitch builds rapport and prevents the uncomfortable "but seriously..." moment that usually follows an 'ice breaker'.

Opening

Planning the opening to your pitch needs much more careful thought than simply introducing yourself and launching in.

Your opening sets the stage, captures the audience's attention and connects through to the close of your pitch.

Timing

Jokes and dramatic openings rely on..... timing, so if you're nervous, avoid high impact openings.

And if all else fails, pause.

Never, Never, Ever

There are a few things to avoid doing during your pitch, apart from the obvious things like turning up in your pyjamas.

Never apologise, make bad jokes, make the audience wait or stick to the script.

And most of all, never take anyone's advice at face value.

SECRET 4

DREAM THE DREAM

The Dream

Your pitch, your idea, was created in a dream world. In order for that dream to become a reality, you need to share that dream with the audience.

What I mean is that your pitch started with an idea. If you got in any way emotionally involved with that idea then you saw it, heard it, felt it and so on. You lived it. For a fleeting moment, that dream became your reality, and you have to draw the audience into that dream so that they can see, hear and feel it through their own perceptions and experiences.

When you begin your pitch, the audience has a preconception about what to expect. If you have followed my advice so far, you will have sent the audience an invitation, and in that invitation you will have influenced the audience's preconception about you and your pitch.

When you begin the main pitch, the part where you're speaking, you have to establish your dream as a shared reality. You need to invite the audience to join and draw them in.

The audience needs to suspend their beliefs and disbeliefs and be prepared to join you in your dream.

Don't Tell Us What to Think... Show Us

Your client doesn't want to know how wonderful you think your product or idea is. They want to find out for themselves.

If you're pitching a physical product, the audience can try out the prototype. They can hold it, use it, see it, feel it and hopefully not break it.

When you're pitching an idea, you don't have that luxury. Fortunately, it's a lazy luxury and you don't need it. You're much better off not having to rely on props and products, so that you can pitch anything to anyone, any time, anywhere. If you have a product to show them too, that's a bonus.

Drawing the audience into your dream allows you to convey far more than you ever could describe in facts, figures and 'benefits'.

If you tell the audience what to think about your product or service, you break rapport and, more importantly, you don't do anything to actively engage them in the learning process that they must go through in order to make a decision.

If you tell the audience that your product is:

☐ Ground breaking

☐ Market leading

☐ Innovative

☐ Best selling

Then you aren't just putting words into their mouths, you're telling them what to think, and you don't like being told what to think, do you? So whilst you might think these words sum up your product perfectly, they actually break the rapport that you have worked so hard to create.

Also, let's say that your idea genuinely is innovative. Who cares? What if the audience doesn't buy innovative ideas? What if they only buy proven ideas? When you get the idea, the dream, into their minds, they will decide what to call it, and as long as what they call it is what they buy, does it matter what that is?

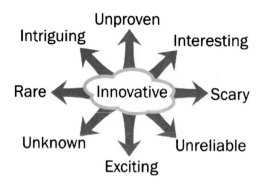

The problem is that words are metaphors, and whilst we have a broadly common understanding of language, our metaphors are sufficiently different that they can break rapport when used carelessly.

4.1 Synonyms

Try this experiment.

Go to 5 people around your office and ask them to give you a synonym (a word with a similar meaning) for the following words:

Professionalism

Innovative

Confusing

Complicated

Free

What did you discover?

What did the person's synonyms tell you about them?

What did their chosen words tell you about their experiences?

Did everyone come up with the same synonyms?

The synonyms were probably different for a very simple reason. In order to generate a synonym, you have to go up to the metaphor that it represents and then down into another word that connects with it.

If people gave you different synonyms, they have different metaphors, which means that they have different life experiences underpinning their understanding of those words.

Therefore, when you tell the audience that your product is innovative, each person accesses a different life experience in order to understand what you're talking about, and the group's involvement in your pitch breaks down. They each go off in a slightly different direction. Some of them will go off in a direction that helps you, some will hinder you. You might think that this can't make a big difference, yet in a highly competitive market, that difference means that you walk out of the door with a "yes", and isn't that worth taking a little extra effort over?

When you are able to convey your dream, in all of its richness and vivid colour, into the minds of the audience and from that, let them draw their own conclusions as to how to describe it, they are selling themselves on their own idea. They have personalised it. They have mixed your words with their own life story. They have become part of your dream.

A Word on Sales... "Enthusiasm"

I know that different 'experts' have different views on sales, on what it is and how you should do it.

One thing that we can say for certain is that if any of them were right, they would have the monopoly on sales training and they would put all of the other experts out of business and retire to a private island in the Caribbean.

So before I head off to the airport, I'd like to share my definition of sales with you.

Sales is the transfer of enthusiasm from one individual to another

This has some important consequences.

Firstly, in order to transfer enthusiasm, you must have some yourself.

Secondly, in order to transfer anything, there must be some kind of relationship in place.

Thirdly, we're presuming that enthusiasm is important in making a good decision and when the buyer has it in relation to your product or service, they are more likely to buy from you.

Having enthusiasm for something means that you are emotionally engaged in it. Enthusiasm means that you are sufficiently engaged to raise your energy level to the point that you want to share how you feel with other people. Enthusiasm is an emotion made for sharing.

I've heard it said that when someone has a good customer experience, they tell two other people, and when they have a bad customer experience, they tell seven other people. Perhaps, as a social species, we like to warn our comrades about possible danger. Or maybe we like to tell war stories, tales of daring and courage, adventures, surviving life threatening perils, such as sub-standard hamburgers or books with spilling mistakes in.

A colleague of mine and his partner recently had a bad experience buying a carpet, which turned out to have a fault in it. The shop owner came for a look. The manufacturer's area manager came for a look. The manufacturer's Directors sent an independent assessor for a look. Everyone agreed that it wasn't right, and something ought to be done about it.

My colleague and his partner have told every single friend and relative they have spoken to about this series of unfortunate events. If the fitting of the carpet had been without incident, then only visitors to their house would have been told, "We've had new carpets fitted", somewhere in between saying, "This looks nice" and being told to take their shoes off.

In Secret Five, Mind Your Language, we'll explore some of the language of enthusiasm. For now, we'll pick up on the non-verbal communication that we talked about in Secret Three.

When you're naturally enthusiastic about something, you can't wait to tell everyone. Your enthusiasm is genuine and infectious. If you believe in your product or service to such a degree that you love telling everyone about it then you're very lucky. If you're selling a product or service that's good, but nothing to get worked up about, then you might need a little help.

4.2 Enthusiasm

Take two pieces of paper.

On one, write the name of something that you are genuinely enthusiastic about.

This is 'A'.

On the other, write the name of something that you are pitching.

This is 'B'.

Stand in front of a clear desk or table and place them in whatever location on the table feels right for you.

Take a moment to think about each one in turn; what it involves, what it represents and so on.

Then, pick up the two pieces of paper and put 'B' where 'A' was. Keep 'A' to one side and concentrate on 'B'.

How does that feel?

What insights did you gain into why you feel the way that you do about 'B'?

This is a non-verbal variation on something we're going to explore more in Secret Five.

Enthusiasm is a state, and you might remember that in Secret Two we talked about the process of 'anchoring' as a basic foundation of learning. Our brains process information through connections, and the more connected something is, the more valuable and important it is.

We've talked about the importance of enthusiasm, and enthusiasm is one of countless emotions that you are capable of experiencing.

What makes an emotional response? In particular, when you recall a memory, how do you know how to feel? Think of something that gives you that sinking feeling, and then think of something that makes you feel warm and fuzzy. How do you know the difference?

You might say, "Well it's a happy memory, so of course it makes me feel good" but it's not quite that simple. When you think of a happy memory, where is the picture? How big is it? How bright is it?

Here's the interesting thing: for many people, happy memories are big, bright and colourful. Unhappy memories tend to be small and dark. Why is this interesting? Think of the implications. It turns out that the emotional label on a memory is not directly related to the content of the memory – it's related to the structure of it. By structure I mean the qualities of the sensory components of the memory, as in these examples:

Sight	Sound
□ Location of image	□ One point/all around
□ Motion/still	□ Loud/soft
□ Colour/black and white	□ Fast/slow
□ Bright/dim	□ High/low pitch
□ Focused/unfocused	□ Clear/muffled
□ One /many images	□ Near/far

Touch	Taste & Smell
□ Location in body	□ Bitter
□ Breathing rate	□ Sweet
□ Temperature	□ Acrid
□ Weight	□ Sharp
□ Intensity	□ Acidic
□ Movement	□ Musty

For example, if you're watching your favourite TV program, you could be watching it on a colour TV, a black and white TV, your laptop, a cinema screen, your phone, through a shop window and so on. The program, the content, is the same but the medium is different, and the medium might make a difference to your viewing experience and enjoyment. The screen size, colour, distance etc. are qualities of the image, and are completely independent of the content or subject of the image.

Every experience that you have ever had arrived through your senses, so everything you have ever seen has taken up your entire field of view and every sound has been as clear as what you are hearing now. So when you think of a time when you felt really hurt or disappointed, why does it look different?

You may never have noticed this before, and that's quite understandable. You probably also didn't notice that your favourite film has a Spanish soundtrack, if you look on the DVD menu. You probably also didn't notice the plates and cutlery used by the last restaurant you ate in.

Imagine that you receive a birthday present wrapped in pink, flowery wrapping paper with the text "You're a cute little angel" on it. Imagine that you receive the same birthday present wrapped in blue paper with footballers on it and the text, "You're an ace striker!". How do you feel differently about those two presents? What about the same present wrapped in plain silver paper? What about plain brown paper? All of these reactions, and you don't even know what the present is yet! Does your reaction to the wrapping paper influence how you feel about the present? What about your feelings towards the person who gave you the present?

Think about some birthday or Christmas presents that you remember receiving as a child. You might even remember how you felt opening those presents. Do you remember the wrapping paper? Do you think it's possible that the way that those presents were wrapped influenced how you felt as you opened them, and that that impression has stayed with you?

There's normally no need for you to notice how you remember memories, because how you feel about the experience is a given, a truth, reality. That experience really did feel like that. Yet you also know that the way you feel about an experience can change over time. So why wait?

Can you think back to an experience where you felt embarrassed? When you picture that event, how do you feel? Does the image look exactly how it looked at the time? Does it seem darker? Smaller? More distant? How do you feel if you make that image bigger? Brighter? Closer?

Can you remember an event which was embarrassing at the time, but as you have talked to friends and family about it, you don't feel so bad, and you might even have seen the funny side.

It's as if the visual and auditory parts of your brain provide the raw data of the memory and some other part of your brain has to package that so that you know how to feel about the memory. You need to be able to remember what the memory means to you so that you know how to respond to it. Also, if a similar event occurs in 'real life', you know how to respond to that, too.

Your brain codes the meaning of a memory through these qualities. The meaning is conveyed outside of the content itself. You could think of these qualities as being information that exists outside of the message that tells the receiver what to do with the message.

Does this sound familiar? Think back to Secret Three where we talked about non-verbal communication. The tonal and visual elements of communication do not, for the most part, carry a message of their own, instead they modify the verbal message.

Some people would argue that this makes the additional information an intrinsic part of the message, because it forms part of the overall meaning, and that's certainly what Mehrabian and Argyle were getting at. They were breaking the overall communication down into the components that they could readily identify. Today, with new tools and techniques, they might have discovered even more aspects of communication.

So your communication has components which are not explicitly part of the message but which modify the message, and your experiences and memories have components which modify their meaning and your responses to them.

So while you may not have noticed before that bad memories tend to be small, dark and distant, now that you have noticed, you might want to do something about it.

4.3 The Structure of Memories

You can try this at home: ask someone to remember a time when they experienced a particular emotional state – anything will do, although strong states are easier to work with.

Go through each of the qualities listed above and find out how your partner structures their memory. Then have them pick a different state and go through the process again, noticing which qualities have changed.

Here are some states that you can try this with:

Surprised	**Confused**	**Anxious**
Argumentative	**Smug**	**Curious**
Worried	**Relieved**	**Enthusiastic**

Compare how they structure a memory differently than you do, for a given state. For example, with a 'surprised' memory, your picture might be large, theirs might be small. Do you notice a connection between the differences and how they feel about the state or event?

Let's say for example that 'enthusiastic' had a picture above eye level, at about arms length, bright and colourful, whilst 'reluctant' had a picture down on the floor, over to the left, dark and colourless.

What if we take the picture of 'reluctant', move it, turn up the brightness and colour, would it become 'enthusiastic'? If you are specific enough about the qualities of the memory, then often the answer is 'yes'.

Handy, isn't it? Think of something in the future that you are not looking forward to. Can you change the qualities of the thought to change your response, so that you actually feel more motivated? Yes you can, very easily. In fact, it's easier to change responses for future events because the events haven't happened yet.

As with anchoring that we discussed back in Secret Two, swapping the qualities of thoughts and memories has two important implications for pitching.

Firstly, you can change the way that you feel about pitching, or a particular client, or a particular project, service or product. You already know that the way you feel is subjective, and logically, you know that you don't have to feel that way. So now you can take control and change the way that you feel, and that changes the way you behave, and that changes the situation in the real world.

Secondly, you can influence the way that your colleagues and clients feel about certain subjects.

Changing States

Imagine that someone in your office handles certain tasks that you are dependent on. They might be an administrator, or someone technical, or this person might even be your manager.

Imagine that, when you ask them to do something for you, they write it on a sticky note and stick it on their desk.

Take a look at their desk and notice where the sticky notes are.

If you don't already have someone in mind, think about someone who writes a 'to do' list, or writes notes on a whiteboard. Look for some visible way of prioritising and organising tasks. Let's say that this person sticks notes to their computer screen, like this:

I'm going to tell you something very important about this person's sticky notes, and you can easily verify what I'm going to tell you, either by observing them or by asking them.

This person's notes and lists may look a mess, but they are in fact perfectly organised.

When you begin to work out their system, you notice that their screen is divided into specific areas.

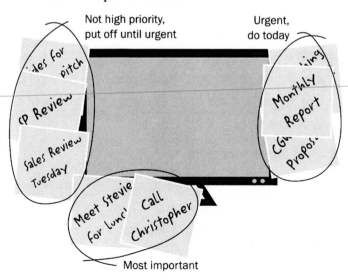

There is a direct correlation between where this person sticks the note for your task and their likelihood of actually completing it for you. So when you watch them write the note and stick it on their screen, you can see how important they think it is, regardless of how much they stress that they will try really, really hard to get it done, just as soon as they can.

Now imagine that you want to make your task a higher priority for them. You go to their desk and you notice that they have placed your note in their low priority area. What do you do with it?

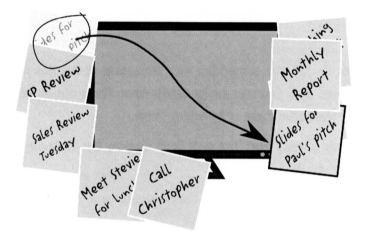

Notice that I haven't moved it to the highest priority, because that would probably be unrealistic. Some people would stick their note right in the centre of the screen, which makes the person simply re-file it back to where it came from. We want to make sure that the new priority stays as it is.

Now let's apply this to your pitch.

Your client also organises both their physical and mental workspace according to some personal, unique and highly organised system. If you can work their system out, just imagine for a moment how you could use that knowledge.

Looking at the client's desk, where does the client put things that they really don't want to deal with, like their tax return or some HR paperwork? Where do they put important items, such as urgent reports? And where do they put things that are valuable to them, such as their family photos?

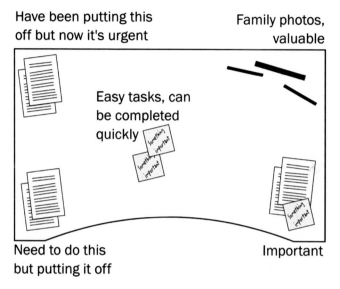

Have been putting this off but now it's urgent

Family photos, valuable

Easy tasks, can be completed quickly

Need to do this but putting it off

Important

Let's translate their physical workspace into an analogous mental workspace.

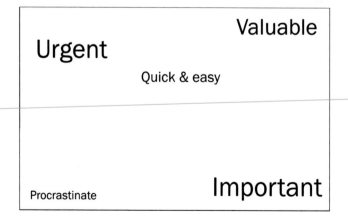

Valuable

Urgent

Quick & easy

Procrastinate

Important

Finally, let's put that mental workspace onto a presentation slide and a page of a proposal.

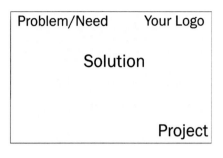
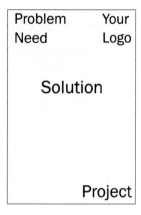

In this example, the 'problem' or 'need' would be a name or symbol for the business problem that the client is trying to solve and the 'project' is a name or symbol for what you are proposing. Your actual solution, the specific thing that the client's decision is based on, is in their 'quick and easy' space, which makes it less likely for them to put it off by moving it into their 'procrastinate' space.

Let's say that your client feels better about big, bright pictures than they do about small, dark pictures. You can see that, if you're going to show computer slides, big bright pictures are a good thing. But, you might also think that you would only ever have big, bright pictures anyway. What's the point of having computer slides with small, dark pictures on?

Would you say anything in your pitch that you wouldn't want your client to feel good about? For example, their current situation, or your competitors? Do you realise that your biggest competitive threat comes not from another supplier but from the client themselves? They always have the option to solve their problems in house, to do it themselves, or to do nothing at all.

Let's piece this puzzle together with an example.

Imagine that you create a presentation to use in your pitch. In your presentation, you have, amongst other things, a slide showing 'current situation', a slide showing 'your solution' and a slide showing 'alternative options'.

The 'current situation' slide comes first. That has smaller, darker images on. Only slightly smaller and darker, though. The client's unconscious mind will understand the connection.

Then, the 'your solution' slide. Big, bright, colourful. You might even have an animation that grows the images as you talk.

Then, the 'alternative options' slide where you offer your client a balanced, neutral assessment of your competitors and the 'do nothing' option. Smaller and darker.

Finally, end with the 'your solution' slide again, and leave that up as you talk about next steps. Big and bright. And getting brighter.

We all like to hear that the weather will be getting warmer and brighter by the weekend, don't we?

Remember, the whole point of improving your pitching skills is leaving absolutely no stone unturned, stacking the odds in your favour and making the most of every opportunity. The best pitchers learn about their client and notice every detail that will help them to gain an advantage over their competitors.

In the old days, that meant just remembering the client's golf handicap and their children's names. It meant noticing details like their family photos, but not knowing why their location was important. It meant getting to know the client, inside out.

By taking advantage of the latest refinements in psychology and sociology, we can begin to attach meaning to the client's behaviour. You can sift through what you have learned about the client and retain what is valuable. Most importantly, you can use what you know to gain an advantage over your competitors.

All things being equal, if a number of potential suppliers are pitching to the client, then any one of them could, on paper, give the client what they want. Why shouldn't that be you? And why would you leave that outcome to chance?

And, if you're sufficiently interested in your own success to be reading this, the chances are that your competitors are too. Which of you is going to gain the advantage by putting this into practice?

Stealing the Space

We've established that locations are important to people.

Have you already had a look around your own work space to see how you broadcast your priorities?

After a couple of unsuccessful attempts at pitching a TV show, I placed my proposal on the producer's desk in the same location as the incumbent supplier's proposal. The client literally said that my proposal was, "in the right area" and my show was commissioned.

Have you already noticed that, when you pitch, you prefer to stand in a particular location, relative to the audience?

Let's say that you're one of a number of people to present or pitch to a particular audience. Let's say that the presenter before you was terrible. Would you stand in the same location?

Let's say that the presenter before you was brilliant. Now where would you stand?

I once advised a nervous client to stand in the same place as a presenter who was confident and engaging. By 'stealing the space', the client said that he felt that he had 'inherited the confidence' of the previous speaker.

Earlier, we talked about lecterns and their effect on rapport. Since lecterns are generally a bad thing because they act as a physical barrier between the speaker and the audience, we can assume that most pitches delivered from behind a lectern are not so good. The lectern is both a physical barrier and a reminder of a poor pitch, so it's twice as important to step out and face your audience.

When you walk into the client's meeting room, the room layout will tell you where every presenter stands. The chairs and table, the whiteboard, the flip charts, even the door and windows will tell you where you should stand.

'Should', that is, if you want to be tarred with the same brush as every other presenter who has stood in that room.

Choosing the location that you want to pitch from is an important part of claiming your territory, and it is an important part of being in control of how you feel, and how you feel directly influences how the audience feels and therefore the outcome of your pitch.

Journey

Think of your favourite film, or a film that you have seen recently. How does it make you feel?

It's not one feeling is it?

It might start by making you feel curious, then surprised, then amused, then surprised, then scared, then relieved, then scared, then relieved, then terrified and so on.

The point is that the director of the film takes you on an emotional journey. The scenes are filmed in a completely different order than that of the final film. Scenes are filmed in multiple locations at the same time. Special effects and music are added in later on. The final product is edited together to create an experience for the viewer that hooks their emotions and doesn't let go until the lights in the cinema come back up.

How does your pitch lead the audience on an emotional journey?

Think back to the pitch design process that we talked about in Secret Two. In the 'Structure' stage, you planned how you want the audience to feel at each point in your pitch.

Let's say that you want the audience to feel 'curious' at the beginning. How do you get someone to feel curious?

Think back to Secret Two. With rapport, all you have to do is be curious yourself. I don't mean act in a strange way, that will probably just raise a few eyebrows. I mean be genuinely curious about where the pitch is going and how much the client is going to enjoy it.

And if you want the client to have fun? Once you're in rapport, just relax and have fun yourself.

Fun

70.9% of corporate buyers said that they would switch suppliers on the basis that the new supplier was more fun[5].

Once you have bought a product or service, what is your main reason for interacting with the supplier after the initial sales process? It's probably to ask a question or to make a complaint.

That's not much fun, is it?

I'm not suggesting you take your client to the fun fair and win them a goldfish, I'm suggesting that every interaction with them has to be upbeat, optimistic, positive and recognise that you are in this together. A problem shared is a problem solved.

---

5   According to a book that I read on guerilla marketing.

Fun is one of a number of states that you might want your audience to experience in relation to your product or service, and while you might make the sales process engaging and enjoyable for the client, a big question for them is going to be how this extends out into the future working relationship.

A client with a budget will be more popular than the last punnet of strawberries at Wimbledon and will be inundated with lunch invitations and offers of corporate entertainment, so while your clients will be only too happy to suck your expenses budget dry, they're not going to spend their money with you just because you show them a good time.

Remember, a client is for life, not just for Christmas.

Your client has no idea how the working relationship is going to work out in the long term, so one of the things you need to do during your pitch, and during the sales process overall, is give the client a compelling glimpse of the future.

The Future's Bright

In Secret Two, we talked about mental rehearsal as a technique for preparing yourself for the pitch.

The technique can equally be used with the client to help them mentally rehearse their future working relationship with you.

You've heard that the future's bright, and you need to make it literally big, bright and colourful.

I'm not talking about the inflated claims that some advertisers make, for example, "The first toothpaste with cooling crystals for freshness to the max". This claim doesn't even end with an exclamation mark, which means that the advertisers are quite serious that you will be totally maxed out with freshness, dude. If I wanted my toothpaste to have cooling crystals in, I would keep it in the freezer.

Inflated claims simply make the client suspicious and cynical. Therefore, you should not claim that the client will continue to have the sales team all over them like a rash once the order is signed. You should not claim that your engineers have world class interpersonal skills. You should not claim that your directors are happy to talk to any customer about any minor problem, day or night. What you should do is set the client's expectations in a way that allows you to meet them. Not exceed them. Meet them.

What I'm talking about is a realistic expectation of the working relationship, communicated in a way that is vivid and compelling.

Rather than spend too long trying to contrive the exact words that you might use to do this, here's a very simple, practical way to do this. Of course, this works for pretty much everything, too.

4.4 Big and Bright

Think about a client who you will be pitching to for new business.

Imagine the working relationship with them.

Is the picture you see big or small? Bright or dark? Near or far? Is it a movie or a still photograph? Is it colourful or grey?

Be aware of the qualities of the image and notice any important information that this gives you, for example, if the picture is small and dark, are you dreading working with the client?

However the picture looked to begin with, make it big, bright, colourful, close and moving.

If you see things in the picture that you don't think are realistic, change them.

Now describe the picture to a friend or colleague.

Ask your friend or colleague to tell you how they feel about the future working relationship that you have just described to them. Ask them what their impression is; did you seem optimistic about the future?

> Do they feel optimistic? What questions do they have about it?

If you are looking at and describing a giant poster in the street, you don't need to say that you're looking up, it's huge, it's colourful and so on. Those qualities are implicit in the way you describe the poster and are therefore more credible.

When you describe your big, bright, colourful, vivid mental image of your working relationship with the client, you don't need to say that it's big, bright and colourful. It will be written all over your face. It will shine through in your voice tone. Your hands will be painting a gigantic, vivid poster. You'll naturally be using all of your communication channels to shout, "Wow! You've got to come and look at this!" to your audience.

One of the things that sales people often do is to try to exceed the customers' expectations. We talked about this in Secret Two. Therefore, if you tell the customer that delivery will be on a certain day, just make sure that it does happen on that day. Think about what the client needs to do to use the product before you rush to get it there a week early.

For example, if it's a new mobile phone, the customer would probably be pleased to receive it a week early. Unless they have to be there to sign for the parcel, so they miss it and have to arrange redelivery. It's better that it comes on the day you said it would.

I recently ordered a new home Internet connection and I asked the person in the supplier's call centre what other discounts I could have. She said that she couldn't give any more discounts, but she could give me the highest speed service at no extra cost for three months. Why would I want that? They're hoping that I get used to the faster service and don't want to be downgraded at the end of the free trial. Still, this sales tactic works for drug dealers, so why shouldn't Internet service providers try it too?

Do not give the client anything to exceed their expectations. This is the hallmark of someone who wants to be liked, someone who is trying to win the client's favour.

4.5 Opportunities

Imagine that you sell computers. You win an order from a new client. When you process the order, the technical department tell you that the model of computer that the client has ordered has just been superseded, and the replacement has a higher specification. You call the client to tell them. Do you say:

A. Great news! I've got an even better deal for you! I spoke to my boss and twisted his arm to let you have a higher 'spec' for the same price!

B. We've just had an order cancelled from another client for a higher spec model than the one you've ordered. Normally we would return them to the manufacturer, but if you ordered a year's maintenance contract, I could let you have them for the same price as the ones you've ordered.

C. Just before I put the order through, I want to check the spec that I'm ordering for you. Do you know that you can get a higher spec model, which would probably give you another couple of years' life on the investment, for only a little more?

If you answered A then you'll do anything to please. If you're in sales, you probably run around a lot more than you need to, and if you manage to hit your sales target at all, it feels like a struggle.

If you answered B then you're doing OK, you see the opportunity. Unfortunately, if the client says "no, thanks" you're left in the awkward position of having to supply the higher spec anyway, and the client will realise that you tried to use it to your advantage.

If you answered C, you are trying to open the conversation again. When the client says that, unfortunately, their budget is fixed, you can offer the client the same price in return for something else that is of value.

A British IT supplier traded advertising space on the client's fleet of lorries for a discount on IT services. If the client is a hotel chain, you could get reduced rates on conference rooms. If the client supplies office furniture, you could get a discount. If the client makes home furnishings, you could trade your discount on the computers for a personal discount on some furniture for your house.

A real sales person uses opportunities like this to reopen the conversation and introduce other variables into the negotiation. They're not trying to be liked. They're trying to do a better deal, both for themselves and for their client.

The point is that good sales people only exceed the client's expectation when that is worth something to the client and can therefore be traded. If all it's worth is to make the client happy, a good sales person makes sure that the client remembers that feeling and associates it with the sales person.

A good sales person, having tentatively reopened the conversation in order to avoid making any firm commitments, might say, "So how would you feel if I could get you a higher spec for the same price?"

Of course, the client can reply with, "Not as good as I'll feel when you give me what I ordered for a lower price!" because the client will assume that a larger discount will be applicable, regardless of the 'spec'.

Therefore, a good sales person would only make such a proposal at the very end of an exploratory conversation, at which point the client might be expected to say, "Great!"

And when the client feels great, the sales person wants to capture that feeling.

How would you achieve that? Anchoring. Secret Three.

I Dreamed a Dream

Everything that you can see around you began as a dream, an idea in someone's mind.

How you convey your dream into your client's mind determines how and when it becomes a reality.

This Secret has dealt with how you convey not information but meaning in your pitch, and the meaning is the basis upon which your audience will make a decision.

We are meaning making machines; we assess huge volumes of sensory data, most of it outside our awareness, and reach an instant conclusion. When we act on that conclusion, we do so with a degree of certainty.

When the meaning and message of your pitch align with your client's certainty, you know you are heading in the right direction.

Secret Brief

The Dream

Your pitch began as a dream, an idea. Your pitch draws the audience into that dream and makes it real.

Don't Tell Us What to Think... Show Us

Don't tell the audience what to think about your pitch because this breaks rapport. Use concepts and metaphors to paint a picture and allow the audience to draw their own conclusions.

A Word on Sales... "Enthusiasm"

Sales is the transfer of enthusiasm from one individual to another, and enthusiasm is infectious. In fact, any strong state is infectious.

Changing States

Not only are states infectious, they each have their own unique characteristics and language that can be used to change them.

Once you have learned to influence and change states, you can borrow them from other people too.

Journey

A pitch is an emotional journey, leading the audience through ups and downs, highs and lows to an action packed ending.

Fun

70.9% of corporate buyers said that they would switch suppliers on the basis that the new supplier was more fun.

The Future's Bright

A big, bright, colourful, vivid future makes almost anything worth having.

I Dreamed a Dream

Everything around you began as an idea, and someone had to pitch those ideas in order to make them a reality.

SECRET 5

MIND YOUR LANGUAGE

The Language of Pitching

We've talked about conveying the meaning of your pitch, so now it's time to communicate the information that the audience needs to support that meaning.

Once you open your mouth to speak, you are, of course, using language to communicate ideas.

As we saw in Secret Four, Dream The Dream, words are a fairly sparse means of communicating rich and vivid information, and so the listener will be filling in a lot of gaps in order to make sense of what you say. Most of those gaps will be filled with your non-verbal communication, and the rest will be filled with the client's preconceptions.

They say that you cannot not communicate, and once you have made an initial connection with someone, you're forever communicating with them. Have you ever jumped to a conclusion when someone didn't call you as promised? They communicated with you by doing absolutely nothing.

Because it's practically impossible to fully describe anything in language alone, we rely on the recipient of our communication to have some knowledge to build upon.

For example, you're walking in the countryside and you need somewhere to stay for the night. There are no hotels nearby, and you can't carry a house around with you. So you need some kind of portable house. Something small, waterproof and light that will give you shelter for the night.

What could it be?

That's right, you're pitching a tent.

Features and Benefits

Traditional sales training advocated selling benefits rather than features. A nice idea in principle, but let down by poor execution.

What sales people most often say is, "Here's the feature, which means that you get this benefit".

It's the wrong way round.

By the time you're half way through describing the feature, the audience is already thinking about the benefit. Otherwise they have no interest in it whatsoever. When you finally get round to the benefit, it will be different to what they had in mind. Even the most subtle difference will break rapport.

Compare these two examples:

"This book contains the seven secrets of successful pitches which means that you can read it quickly and easily"

"This book gives you everything you need to know because it has all seven secrets of successful pitches in it"

It's a subtle difference, and it's enough to tip the balance in your favour. It helps you to keep the rapport that you will have worked so hard to establish, and it keeps the audience in the world of the idea without slipping back into the harsh reality that they're sitting in a dark room wondering where all the chocolate biscuits have gone.

With "Feature Means Benefit", the audience has already imagined a benefit by the time you have finished describing the feature, and because that will be different to how you describe the benefit, the result is a subtle disagreement which breaks rapport.

With "Benefit Because Feature", the audience accepts the benefit first as something worth having and is then waiting to find out how that benefit can be achieved.

5.1 Features and Benefits

Think of your own product, or pick something that's in front of you at the moment.

Get a piece of paper and write out six features that it has. Then write out the six benefits of those features.

Finally, ask two other people what they think the benefits of those features might be and write those down too.

Make sure you write down exactly the words that each person uses – that's the key to why this works. It's important that you discover for yourself that different people will interpret the features differently.

Here's an example for you. I'm currently typing on a computer keyboard, so I'll use that to demonstrate what I mean.

Feature	Benefit 1	Benefit 2	Benefit 3
Black	It looks nice	It's easy to keep clean	It matches my screen
QWERTY layout	I can find the keys	It's the most common	I can touch type
Made of plastic	It's light	It's easy to clean	It's cheap to buy
USB connector	It plugs into any computer	It's adaptable	I don't have to look for the connector
Rubber feet	It doesn't slide on the desk	It makes it quieter to type on	It doesn't scratch the desk
Two shift keys	Good for left or right handed use	I can brag to my friends about it	It has a spare in case one breaks

Yes, there will be many common themes in the benefits that your colleagues suggest, yet it's the differences that are most valuable, because they contain the keys to making your pitch stand head and shoulders above your competitors' pitches.

WIIFM?

Why are there differences in the benefits that people attribute to a product's features? Because each person is interpreting the feature through their own 'WIIFM?' filter.

This special filter allows you to ask "What's In It For Me?" whenever you're presented with a fact or decision. You might also experience this as the "So What?" filter, the "And Why Should I Care?" filter and the "Don't Tell Me What To Think" filter.

Our 'WIIFM?' filter evaluates incoming information to judge it against our own beliefs and perception of the world. It protects us from accepting other people's beliefs too readily. Unfortunately, it also prevents us from accepting new information too.

You know that your 'WIIFM?' filter is working properly when someone gives you advice about a problem and you answer, "Yeah, yeah, I know", or, "You don't understand", or you just nod and say thank you, but really you're thinking, "What do they know?"

Anything that you don't agree with just bounces off the 'WIIFM?' filter.

This means that if you present by talking facts at your audience, it doesn't matter how true or well researched you think those facts are, some people will find them contentious, simply as a result of the way you have presented them.

The 'WIIFM?' filter intercepts incoming information and validates it against your own beliefs before you can act upon it. You can experience this as anything from a full blown preconception about someone to the sensation of not being able to see your car keys when they are right in front of you.

This is a very valuable skill, because without it you wouldn't be able to check new information against what you know to be true in your experience. We evolved the ability to learn and generalise new experiences for our own survival, for example learning that if one lion was dangerous, they probably all were.

Do you remember your parents telling you that roads or strangers are dangerous? As an adult, you know that it's a generalisation, yet you also know that it's a useful one.

What other generalisations have you learned which aren't so useful?

More to the point, what generalisations have your audience learned which stand in the way of you getting your message across.

The good news is that you don't have to struggle to force your ideas past the filter. You have to tease out what is already in there – the desire to acquire the benefit of your product, even though the audience doesn't yet know how that will be possible.

When you begin to notice how the audience interprets the features of your product, you will realise just how much you can discover about their inner world; their motivations, interests, fears and, most importantly, their buying criteria.

Firstly, you can make sure that the people you're pitching to are in as receptive a state as possible before you begin. We talked about ways that you can do this in the Secret Two.

For example:

- Use every opportunity to communicate with the audience prior to the presentation
- Frame the presentation - let the audience know what to do
- Answer the audience's unspoken questions
- Build rapport with the audience

Secondly, you can use the two simple, everyday forms of communication which will bypass the 'WIIFM?' filter completely.

What's that? You can bypass the audience's 'WIIFM?' filter, their preconceptions and their generalisations altogether? How might that be possible?

I was pitching to a new client recently via teleconference, which is not an ideal medium to work in. I felt that I was struggling to get my message across, so I began to give them examples of other clients I had worked with and situations where, as The Pitch Doctor, I had made a measurable impact on a client's ability to succeed. In answer to their questions, I simply told amusing stories that got the message across. By the time I finished my pitch, the client said that it was the most entertaining presentation they had ever experienced, and they awarded me the contract. Now, I'm not telling you this to show off, I'm telling you because I was in a situation where I felt the pitch was not going well and I adapted to the client and in doing so, gave you a clue about one of these simple communication methods that will bypass the client's 'WIIFM?' filter.

These two valuable forms of communication are stories and questions.

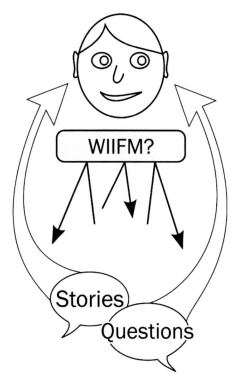

Questions

How do questions bypass the audience's preconceptions?

Well, questions don't convey any information, do they?

Questions don't carry instructions, do they?

Questions definitely can't influence the way you think, because you're not the kind of person who would be influenced so easily, are you?

A structure of language which you hear as a question puts you into a certain frame of mind, ready to search for and give an answer. Over time, the right balance of questions will guide your audience into a receptive, open minded and interactive state which is ideal for learning and therefore for pitching.

We hear questions when:

☐ The speaker's voice pitch rises towards the end of a sentence

☐ A sentence starts with a word such as why, when, where, how, what, which, who, if, is, could, would, will, won't, might, may, can, etc.

☐ A statement ends with a tag question, such as couldn't it, don't they, do we, can it, etc.

It's rarely wise to position yourself as a the absolute expert who is going to give the audience all the answers. It's generally useful to think of your role as being to help the audience to explore the questions, and for them to formulate their answers. People rarely ask a question in order to get a straight answer.

Asking questions about your presentation subject can be a very effective way to ensure the audience has all the information they need to make an informed decision.

5.2 Questions

Can you deliver the opening part of your pitch using only questions?

What effect would that have?

What questions would you ask?

Could you practice that right now?

Stories

Listen to any conversation and you will hear a combination of:

- ☐ Belief statements – which sometimes sounds like facts

- ☐ Questions – for many different reasons

- ☐ Narrative – which gives characters and sequence

Human beings communicate with each other in a narrative. We don't communicate using factual statements alone; they are linked by a narrative, which includes characters – who did what to who – and a sequence in time, so that we can recreate the situation mentally.

We learn by observing and copying, and we even have special connections in our brains called Mirror Neurons which reproduce in our own bodies what we see other people doing. These Mirror Neurons allow children to copy behaviour and also to learn emotions and empathy.

If you want to find out more about Mirror Neurons, just type "Mirror Neurons Gallese Goldman" into your favourite Internet search engine and you'll find the original research on the subject.

What happens when there is no primary experience to copy? What happens when you can't see the consequences of ignoring your Mother's advice about crossing the road? Your Mother tells you a story and you enact it in your mind. Imagination is a close substitute for the real thing, and stories are the gateway to the fundamental process of human learning.

For example,

"Eggs are good for you"

"Really? Why?"

"Well my friend was telling me that they've done some research…"

As one person is talking, anyone listening is translating their words back into the original sensory experience. Of course, they can't translate it into exactly the original, so they are substituting their own experiences and references in order to make sense of it. The person listening to the story puts themselves in it. As they empathise, they 'get the message'.

What does this mean for you?

For a start, it means that the more narrative you use, the easier you are to listen to.

Secondly, it means that the richer your narrative, the more accurate are the pictures you create in your audience's mind.

Thirdly, when I ask people what qualities they associate with excellent presenters, one which always comes out is that the presenter knew a lot about their subject. When I ask how they knew that the presenter knew a lot – they told stories.

Narrative communication – storytelling - is vital, it's natural, you already do it and to be an excellent pitcher you need to do more of it, purposefully.

Right now, you communicate in many ways that already fit this form, including:

☐ Anecdotes

☐ Case studies

☐ Reports

☐ Any description of an event

5.3 Stories

Set aside some time at work, perhaps ten minutes, to listen to stories. Try not to get drawn into them, instead just sit back and observe. Monday morning is an ideal time to do this because you can sit at your desk, pretending to read a document, listening to your colleagues' stories of their weekend antics.

Pay attention to the stories and, in particular, notice what images pop into your mind as you listen. Notice how the stories engage you, even if you have no specific interest in them. Why do you think this is?

The Elevator Pitch

Someone recently asked me, "How do I squeeze a thirty minute pitch into three minutes?"

Of course, the answer is that you can't.

Many presentation experts offer you a language structure for the 'Elevator Pitch', enabling you to cram your name, product, benefits and a call to action all into one sentence.

Instead of trying to cram your sales pitch into as short a delivery as possible, I want you to change your focus. Instead of pitching to win the business, pitch to win a chance to pitch. Your three minutes has to buy you the next thirty. Therefore, never, never, never, never ever try to cram all of your most fabulous ideas and compelling USPs into three minutes, or into any length of time for that matter. Instead, focus on how that initial three minutes is the trailer for the movie, the hook that leaves them saying "Call me" instead of "erm.. well it was nice meeting you".

Think of the elevator pitch as a trailer for the main feature. You might even practice your elevator pitch and use it as the introduction to your main pitch, just like a newspaper headline gives you a reason and motivation to read the full story.

If you are remembering the importance of rapport, you'll spend the first of those three minutes getting enough rapport that the next two minutes have the maximum value and impact.

I was once travelling to an important pitch and found myself in the elevator with a man who had just been for a run. I asked him about his run, we talked about training for Marathons and then we both got out of the elevator.

In the meeting room, we had to wait for the CEO to arrive. After a few minutes, guess who walked in? The CEO said, "Sorry to keep you all waiting, I just had to go for a quick run". The sales director began to introduce us and the CEO said, "We've already met".

This is such a vital skill for the professional presenter, not only for the chance meeting in the elevator but in any pitching situation, because you can generally guarantee that you won't have the amount of time that you thought you were going to have.

Let's say the client has given you an hour, so you turn up with your laptop and the presentation that you have spent weeks working on. You stand up at the front of the room, having rehearsed the timing to the second, and the client says, "We're a little pushed for time today because we have to go to a meeting, you know how it is, any chance you could give us your presentation in 10 minutes?" On top of this, you know that your competitors all had their full hour.

"Oh my God!", the voice in your head screams, "How am I going to get through all this in ten minutes?"

Now, take a moment to put yourself in this position and think about what you would do. Seriously, put the book down for a moment and think about what you would do before you read any further.

Would you:

1. Skip through the slides as fast as you can, stopping occasionally when you get to a really important one.

2. Say, "Well that's impossible, you have to give me an hour as you promised".

3. Say, "That's no problem, I know you're busy. Why don't we reschedule so that we all have the time we need to give this our full attention?"

4. Introduce yourself and then jump straight to the summary and questions.

5. Close your laptop, smile and say, "In that case, what can we talk about in the next 10 minutes that will give you all you need to make a decision?"

First of all, I'm fairly certain that this has already happened to you, so what did you do? What do you think would have been a better way to handle the situation?

Option A is very bad indeed. You have allowed the audience to take control and you will ensure that nothing is memorable apart from the fact that you rushed through your slides and said nothing of any interest. You won't win any respect by doing this.

Options B and C are interesting. You're certainly taking control of the situation, as long as you stand your ground. The audience might respect your stand, just don't expect to be invited back, though.

These responses, whilst authoritative, don't take into account Secret One, It's All About Them. That doesn't mean that you have to do what the audience says, it means that you need to focus on them. If you want your hour because you're so proud of your presentation that you want the time to show it then you have prioritised your presentation above the outcome for the pitch itself – what you want the audience to do.

In this situation, a smart pitcher will smile and mentally rub their hands together, because a 10 minute pitch is going to be far more impactful and memorable than your competitors' hour long monologues. If you're on last, that's even better. If your time is short because your competitors ran over, even better. You demonstrate flexibility and control, and you also demonstrate real knowledge of your subject because you can repackage your ideas to take advantage of any situation.

Given 10 minutes, you should aim to be using 5 of those for your pitch. That doesn't seem like a long time, and in fact it isn't, but it's more than enough time to get across your core message.

Option D therefore allows you to 'cut to the chase', to get across the key points that you have already collected together in your summary. At any point during your presentation you can jump to the summary and there are the key points, ready and waiting for you.

Option E puts the emphasis on the audience again. If they want to cut your time down, they can tell you what their priority is. One problem with this approach is that the audience don't always know what their priority is, because they don't always know what they're looking for. If you believe that they do know then this approach can be very powerful.

Remember, a pitch is not a one way communication. Given an hour or ten minutes or even one minute, your focus must not be on cramming as much information into the audience as possible, because they can't take it all in anyway. We'll come back to this later.

The important point is that when you walk in the door expecting an hour, or half an hour, or whatever has been agreed, you should fully expect that to change and have a plan in place, not just to cope with it but to take full advantage of the opportunity.

When you have prepared your pitch and you're getting ready to deliver it, here is a checklist that you can use to make sure you're prepared for any last minute schedule changes.

This is also an important checklist for focusing your attention on the outcome for the pitch.

You'll also find a ready made checklist to download from The Pitching Bible website, www.thepitchingbible.com.

Preparation

- ☑ What is your outcome for your pitch?
- ☑ What do you want the audience to do?
- ☑ What is the most important thing to get across to them?
- ☑ If you have the full time you expect, how will you do that?
- ☑ If you have only half that time, how will you do that?
- ☑ If you have only 5 minutes, how will you do that?

You Know How...

Think about stand up comedians who start a routine with "You know how..."

Yes! I know exactly how! Oh my God, that happened to me! I have hairs in my plug hole! My kettle makes a noise like that! I wear shoes too!

Yes, we all have those same experiences. They're just not particularly funny until we all sit in a big room, get drunk and listen to someone else talk about them. We all like to share in the social bonding experience of agreeing that the buses are unreliable and that our kitchens are trying to kill us.

The comedian builds a routine on those experiences.

You can build your pitch on them.

State the Obvious

My son Sam gazed up at a man who was almost seven feet tall and said, "Wow! It must be fantastic to be so tall".

Often, presenters fear insulting the audience's intelligence, so they avoid stating the obvious.

In fact, stating the obvious is important in developing rapport.

Now, I know that it seems obvious to say that you're reading this book, but it's worth saying anyway because I don't want to make any assumptions. For example, someone else might be reading it to you. I find it fascinating that I'm sitting here, at my computer keyboard, and you're there, reading or hearing these words. It's as if I'm writing a personal letter, from me to you, isn't it? When do you think you'll find the time to write back to me?

Stating the obvious draws the audience into your world.

For example, if you thank the audience at the beginning of your pitch, you can either say, "Thank you for coming", or you can say, "Thank you for your time, I know you have travelled to be here".

The second version makes a statement which everyone can agree with, unless they live in the presentation room. The effect of this is a subtle alignment of rapport, and it is a very important step in gaining a high level of group rapport for your pitch.

You can begin your pitch with universal truths, and you can also wrap those truths in questions.

For example, let's say that you want to use a cat to illustrate a point, and you want to relate this directly to the audience, so you can say, "Does anyone here have a cat? If not, do you know someone who has a cat? Have you all at least seen a picture of a cat?"

The first question elicits a response, a yes or no. The second gathers more of the audience into the 'yes' group, and the third question can be spoken with a little exasperated humour, which lets the remaining people know that they are safe and normal.

If one person answers, "no!" to the last question, in an attempt to heckle you and grab control, you can say, "then how do you know what a cat is?" and then continue regardless of their reply, or if you prefer you can enter into a conversation with the heckler and take up time that you could have been using for your pitch.

Agreement builds rapport. In the world of improvised comedy, one of the cardinal rules is to never disagree. Performers must always build on each others' ideas, never kill them. You may have watched children playing 'make believe' games and arguing with each other when they don't follow this rule.

The children's game might go like this:

"I'm a doctor"

"I'm a fighter pilot."

"You can't be a fighter pilot, they don't belong in a hospital."

"This is a flying hospital in a jet fighter."

"No it isn't, it's a hospital in New York and I'm a famous brain surgeon. You can be my patient."

"No, you're my co-pilot."

"No I'm not."

Each child has its own imaginary world, and is unwilling to join the other in theirs, or even to merge the two worlds together.

The improvised comedy performance, on the other hand, might go like this:

"I'm a doctor."

"And I'm a fighter pilot."

"And I'm having a fantastic time in your flying hospital. Where are we going?"

"We're flying to New York, Doctor, so that you can perform a life saving operation."

"That's right, a brain surgery operation that will save the life of this banana."

"It's so wonderful that you're a famous brain surgeon, what is the best part of your job."

"It's flying around in flying hospitals like this one. Say, could I try flying it for a while?"

And so on...

The 'build on' rule brings the performers together in the same world, and the bizarre nature of that world creates the humour.

When you're pitching, you are inviting the audience to suspend their beliefs and join you in your imaginary world. In the next Secret, we'll be talking more about how to communicate your imaginary world to the client, so for now we'll concentrate on building rapport to draw the audience in.

Stating the obvious, or stating universal truths, is an excellent way to build rapport. It does not insult the audience as long as you're not speaking as if you know something that the audience doesn't.

Phrases such as, "It seems obvious, yet...", or, "Many people find that...", or, "You might already know that..." soften the statement, making it more acceptable.

The danger area is where something seems obvious, so you stress, "obviously...", or "we all know that...", as if anyone who doesn't know is an idiot.

Even if it's something that you think everyone in the audience should know, you can guarantee that at least one person doesn't, or at least thinks that they don't.

Ask a hundred advertising executives if they know what AIDA stands for, and 99 will say, "Of course I do, everyone knows that", and one will say, "Erm, I think so. But I can never remember if the D is Decision or Direction". By acting as if everyone knows, you alienate that one person.

To build rapport at the start of your pitch, you might consider using statements like these:

- ☐ I appreciate you have all made the time to be here
- ☐ Thank you for coming, I know you've travelled to be here
- ☐ It's good to see you all here today
- ☐ I know some people couldn't be here today
- ☐ Now that you're all sitting down...
- ☐ There is water on the table for you
- ☐ I'm here today to...

Alternatively, you can use questions. You're not necessarily looking for interaction with the audience, as that could be disruptive.

Ideally, your audience will respond internally, feeling agreeable and perhaps nodding and smiling with the occasionally murmur of agreement.

For example:

- ☐ Do you want to get some water before I begin?
- ☐ Are you sitting comfortably?
- ☐ Can you hear me clearly?

- ☐ Can you see me OK if I stand here?

- ☐ Can you see the screen OK?

- ☐ Are you ready for me to begin?

- ☐ Can I check some points before I begin?

You can also use similar questions throughout your pitch, to check and deepen rapport from time to time.

- ☐ Do you see?

- ☐ Is that clear?

- ☐ Does that add up?

- ☐ Does that make sense?

- ☐ Is that right?

- ☐ Do you agree?

Getting a Feel For Language

How many ways do you hear people say, "I understand"?

Do these sound familiar?

I get it	I can grasp that
I see	That sounds right
I hear you	I'm with you
That's crystal clear	I dig
That's clear as a bell	Looks great

When you hear these, you probably translate them all into a confirmation of understanding, rather than paying attention to the particular words used.

In fact, the specific words that a person uses tell us whether they are primarily thinking in images, sounds or feelings.

Richard Bandler and John Grindler, the co-developers of NLP, noticed that the excellent communicators who they studied listened and responded to the sensory language of the client they were working with. They acted as if "I see" meant that the client literally could see something that, to them, made everything clear.

Here are those phrases again, with their associated sensory system:

I get it	Feel
I see	See
I hear you	Hear
That's crystal clear	See or Hear
That's clear as a bell	Hear
I can grasp that	Feel
That sounds right	Hear
I'm with you	Feel
I dig	Feel
Looks great	See

All of this is useful, not in categorising people, but in communicating with them more effectively. You may have heard people labelled as 'visual' as if they are only able to understand pictures. In fact, everyone uses all of their senses. Imagine listening to a presentation in a language that you can speak, but not fluently. You translate in your head as much as you can, but after a while you can't help letting your mind wander as you get tired. The same thing happens even when you communicate using the same language, so we are talking about a degree of refinement here which will add to and enhance your pitching skills.

Here are some more sensory specific words that you can use.

Visual	See	Vision	Sharp
	Picture	Outlook	Background
	Look	Bright	Shine
	Watch	Clear	Reflect
	Perspective	Focus	Magnify
Auditory (Tonal)	Listen	Quiet	Whistle
	Hear	Amplify	Whine
	Sound	Tell	Roar
	Noise	Resonate	Silent
	Loud	Clear	Tone
Auditory (Verbal)	Say	Think	Ask
	Speak	Reason	Instruct
	Tell	Know	Read
	Question	Logical	Dialogue
	Chatter	Interpret	Translate
Kinaesthetic	Feel	Push	Down
	Touch	Embrace	Ache
	Grab	Warm	Gut
	Hold	Cold	Queasy
	Contact	Sinking	Shaky

Back in Secret Three, we were talking about eye movements and how they relate to a person's thought processes. In fact, these sensory thought processes are evident in many more ways, only one of which is a person's language.

5.4 Sensory Language

When you next watch the news on TV, or listen to it on the radio, pay attention to the unscripted interviews. Listen out for people using these words. Notice how their language comes alive with a new depth and meaning as you realise how literal these words are, and how the person is describing their inner experience.

Of course, you can try this with real people too, it's just that people on TV don't seem to mind as much when you stare at them.

Once you have a feel for the sensory words that people use, make a note of your colleagues' preferences and begin to respond to them using words that match their preference. Notice the response you get.

Finally, try deliberately mismatching. For example, if someone has a strong visual preference, use kinaesthetic words and notice what happens.

You might be wondering how to use this.

Let's say that you meet a client and he says, "Look, I'm interested in seeing what we could work on together. I think you've got an interesting perspective on our business problems and I think you can help bring some focus to what we're working on. Send me a proposal and we'll look it over."

Well, that's screaming 'visual' language, isn't it?

So you write your proposal using as much visual language and as many graphs and illustrations as you can, yes?

Not quite.

You know that one person, perhaps the decision maker, has a preference for visual thinking. But you have to presume that other people are still involved in the decision, so you write your proposal to have a balance of language and then write your covering letter, addressed to him, with a bias towards visual language.

A person's choice of language and their preferred thinking 'mode' also ties in with something that we're going to explore in Secret Six; learning styles.

Vaguely Specific

Milton Erickson was a Hypnotherapist in Arizona. He can perhaps be credited as the person who made hypnotherapy acceptable in western medicine, using it to help patients that other therapists had declared 'incurable'. Erickson was even able to help Cancer sufferers relieve their pain, simply by telling them stories. Milton Erickson suffered from polio in his early life and took that as an opportunity to spend many long hours paying attention to the effect that words had on people in the conversations that he overheard.

Other experts[6] have since studied Erickson's therapeutic work and have discovered certain consistent patterns which tie into the way that we organise our thoughts and behaviour.

If you listen to any statement or speech prepared by a politician, you will hear a lot of Milton language. For example:

"People will understand that the solutions to these kinds of problems are to be found not in the past but in the future, and everyone will appreciate what a difficult task this can be. You can also be certain that the government you have now is in a far better position than any other to tackle these problems and to resolve them in a way that is economical, effective and respectful to the local community."

Does that sound familiar? Perhaps you remember hearing that before, about asylum seekers, or social housing problems, or local policing policy? Actually, I just made it up.

Milton language is a vague framework within which the listener can

6   See the Bibliography in the Appendix for books on this subject

place their own meaning. If someone tells you that you will be richer if you make a certain decision, you may or may not agree depending on whether money is important to you or not. If they say that you will enjoy even more of the things that are so important to you, you can only make sense of the sentence if you insert something of importance to you. The sentence, whilst sounding vague when we analyse it in this way, actually becomes totally unique and personal to each listener.

In this way, politicians, business leaders and storytellers can communicate directly with every listener or reader in a very personal and individual way.

Presuppositions

Example: "I'll do that after I win this contract"

Response: "How do you know you'll win that contract?"

Presuppositions are the components of the sentence which must be held true in order for the sentence to be grammatically correct. The presupposition works at the unconscious level at which your brain parses language, ready to be decoded and translated into meaning, therefore a presupposition is accepted as true even before you consciously understand what has been said.

When we process language, we process all meanings and hold them temporarily until one stands out by fitting the context of the information. Therefore, presuppositions are a very powerful influence tool.

☐ When this project fails I'll say 'told you so'

☐ It will be easier when he leaves

☐ What will the next reorganisation bring?

☐ When are you leaving?

☐ Who are you going to fire next?

☐ You always enjoy pitching once you're a few minutes into it

☐ Once you make a start you'll find it easy

Modal Operators

Modal operators are words which modify verbs. What we're interested in is the way in which they modify verbs that are in the future tense, in other words actions which the client has not yet taken but which they are thinking about.

Imagine that, at some point in the future, you will find yourself at the shops. Right now, you could speak about this event in a number of ways, for example:

- ☐ I am going to the shops

- ☐ I could go to the shops

- ☐ I will go to the shops

- ☐ I ought to go to the shops

- ☐ I need to go to the shops

The differences between these examples may be subtle or they may be obvious, so just take a moment to go back and picture what each example brings to mind for you. Compare the differences between each example.

Now imagine that a colleague says, "I'm going to prepare for tomorrow's pitch". What do you infer from that?

What if they say, "I ought to prepare for tomorrow's pitch"?

One suggests action, the other suggests procrastination.

It's easy to say, "It's just words", but remember that words are a superficial symptom of our inner emotional state. Words give away secrets that we would rather keep to ourselves, and I'm sure you can think of instances where you have ignored someone's odd choice of words to your detriment.

A common example is when you ask someone to do something for you and they say, "I'll try". When it turns out that they haven't done it, are you really surprised? Or do you tell yourself that "you should have known better"?

An emotional state has its own vocabulary. The words you use, your voice tone and the things you talk about are influenced by, and can influence, your state, and they reveal your true thoughts and intentions.

When our thoughts easily become actions, we are in a motivated state. Sometimes, we allow our thoughts to dissipate without translating into behaviour, or we think about something that we know we have to do, but we don't want to do it.

Think about something that you do easily – something that you can always find time for or that you only have to think about in order to do it. What do you say to yourself as you think about it?

- ☐ Can
- ☐ Will
- ☐ Want
- ☐ Am

Now think about something that you're really good at almost getting round to. Something that is your job, or that needs doing, but you really don't want to do it, so you always find a way to avoid it. What do you say to yourself as you think about it?

- ☐ Ought
- ☐ Should
- ☐ Must
- ☐ Need

Do you notice a pattern here? Is it possible to change the words we use in order to influence state and behaviour?

5.5 Motivation

Take something that you need to do, such as some paperwork. Pay attention to how you talk to yourself about it. If, for example, you say, "I really ought to do that today" then actively change the words. Say out loud, "I am going to do that today".

Of course, you haven't done it yet, it is in the future and is therefore still an uncertainty. We can make the effect even more powerful by shifting it into the past:

"By the end of the day I will have done that"

Now we have the problem that "the end of the day" is not very specific. Which day? When exactly does it end? We can go one better:

"By the time I walk out of the door to go home today, I will have done that"

Stand up. Look up. Take a deep breath. Smile. Think about something you really love doing and really enjoy. Now say in a confident, musical voice:

"By the time I walk out of the door to go home today, I will have done that"

Now take something that you know you should do less of.

Sit down. Look down. Now say in a nervous, flat voice:

"I really ought to do that soon"

What do you notice about how you're thinking about these two tasks or activities?

I know what you're thinking… "If I can use this to manage my own state of motivation, could I use it with other people?"

This is a verbal version of the exercises that you completed in Secret Four where you swapped pieces of paper around an imaginary workspace and changed the qualities of your memories.

Listen carefully to the words that someone uses when they talk about something they really enjoy doing. Then make sure you use those exact words back to them when you talk about what you want them to do.

For example, when someone talks about something they had to finish off at work they might say, "I kept telling myself that I really should do it, I finally ran out of time and had to finish it off before coming here tonight". When they talk about going shopping at the weekend they might say, "so I said to myself 'Ooh! I've just got time to pop into town'".

Now you have everything you need, so you say to them, "I do appreciate that you should take some time to think this over before you make a decision. I know it's important so I'm not going to rush you. Of course, if you just think to yourself, "Ooh! That's exactly what we need, I want to go ahead" then that's fine too because I know that time is always short."

Previously, I advised against making social small talk with the client. Even when you make business small talk prior to your pitch you can glean the information you need from the client. By getting the client to talk about what they have going on at work and making sure they give you examples of events they're looking forward to and events that they're not, you will hear their modal operators. If they are working on other projects and you can get them to talk about decisions they've made, they will also tell you the modal operators that they use to talk about a decision that they're happy with. Imagine, if the client said that they had been putting a project off for a while but then they thought to themselves, "It's time to do something with this, I can get it done", then guess what you're going to say in the summary to your pitch?

The most important thing, as always, is to notice the words the other person uses, and use their words. Yours might make sense to them, or they might have the opposite effect. For example, 'need' motivates some people and stops others because it implies rules, and some people automatically follow rules whereas others automatically question them, so always pay attention to the person you want to develop a relationship with.

Ambiguity

In Secret Three, we talked about the concept of tonal ambiguity. When you're trying to understand what someone is saying to you, it's very important to choose the right meaning for the sound of the word, for example:

- Right, write or rite
- See or sea
- Sight or site
- Look or luck
- Annoys or a noise
- By, bye or buy
- Sell or cell
- Wait or weight
- Match (a game, a fire lighter or a comparison)
- Lettuce, letters or let us

For example, what does red mean?

Does it mean stop? Or does it mean ripe? Or does it mean 'paper jam'?

Or does it mean that you have looked at and understood some written text?

In the South of England, in a town called Reading (pronounced Redding), there is a literacy school called, 'The Reading School of Reading'.

What about write? Or right? Or rite?

Wait? Weight?

A hypnotherapist might say:

"You can feel the weight in your hands, and you can feel the weight in your feet, and you can feel the wait for the moment that you can let go and relax"

At the end of a sales pitch, a sales person might say:

"Make sure you have a pen, because in a moment I'm going to ask you to right now fill in an order form"

There are also syntactic ambiguities:

- You *see, for yourself,* one copy is often not enough

- That concludes the pitch for *my product. Is the one you're going to choose* based on the pitches you have seen today, or will there be another stage in the process?

Tonal ambiguities work in spoken communication, and if you try to use them in writing, they just seem very strange. Some people selling self-help products write their websites with tonal ambiguities, and it really doesn't work very well.

Syntactic ambiguities work much better in written text than tonal ambiguities do.

At this point, you might be wondering if I have used any hidden ambiguities or embedded commands to influence you in reading this book. The Pitch Doctor for your next conference or corporate event would, of course, be a very good idea and I would be flattered, but if that is something you're interested in doing then you would decide that for yourself, haven't you? So nothing that I could say here or anywhere else would you find such a tempting offer?

Only the most open and above-board language is used here in this book. Now, to avoid disappointment, because I do get a lot of requests to speak at conferences and corporate events so make sure you let me know the dates as soon as possible so I can let you know that I can make it. A great event is really worth planning well in advance, isn't it?

And I would never do anything like that, except to demonstrate the principles to you, because, if you're reading this, you must be the kind of independent thinker who would never be influenced and you never, ever buy anything just because of advertising or peer pressure. Don't worry about it too much, as I do not advocate using these methods alone. Only use them with friends or colleagues and experiment for yourself. Always, always test internally before sending anything out to your client, and if your friends or colleagues feel that something is awkward or too obvious, your client will think so too, which is counter-productive and can potentially damage your reputation.

What works best of all is being clear and direct about the message you want to put across, and using methods like this to add an extra layer of impact to your message.

You cannot convince your client to buy your product or service if it is not fundamentally something that they need. If you do, they'll just feel bad about their decision and resent you, and that is not a good situation to be in. You've hit your sales target but your customers would never buy from you again.

Commands

A command is an instruction. If pitching was as easy as just telling the client to buy from you, you wouldn't need my help. Fortunately, pitching isn't that easy, and the client doesn't always follow instructions, because they have their own opinions and experiences.

Therefore, we need ways to get the message across which are less confrontational than a command whilst more powerful than a tentative suggestion.

Direct Commands

We've talked about questions and stories, and the simplest way to get someone to do something is to tell them to do it.

"Pass me the salt, please darling"

"Please let me have your attention for a moment while I make an important announcement"

"Please make your way down to the front entrance where your car is waiting"

Direct commands are the simplest form of command, and as such are easily intercepted by your 'WIIFM?' filter. You can respond with "erm... no thanks". Or worse still, "Why?"

There are other ways to give someone a command. None of these methods is guaranteed to work, and all of them leave control with the client. You will not be able to get someone to do something against their will, but when all other things are equal, these methods can tip the balance in your favour. For example, if the client is weighing up two proposals, one of them yours and one from your competitor, and they just can't choose between them, subtle methods such as these can make a significant difference to the outcome.

The client might say, "Either of the two proposals gave us what we need, and in the end we just felt that your pitch was stronger. I can't put my finger on why, call it intuition."

Embedded Commands

Sometimes, people ask me where you can buy another copy of The Pitching Bible, and I tell them that it's easy, you just go into any book shop and ask. You see, for yourself, one copy is often not enough and it's good to have one to make notes in and another to enjoy it as much as you want to, tell all your friends, and enjoy it together. Can't you?

An embedded command is an instruction that is embedded within a longer language structure. The simplest form is to embed "Enjoy my pitch" into "I hope that you enjoy my pitch". A more complex form is to embed the command into "I was a bit nervous this morning but my friend told me to just relax and enjoy my pitch, so I'll do my best".[7]

Embedded commands can be quite complex, so they go hand in hand with something called analogue marking, where some kind of non-verbal stress is placed on the command to mark it out. The stress should be very, very subtle, as it is a signal to the listener's unconscious mind, and not something that you want them to be consciously aware of.

The first paragraph in this section had a number of embedded commands in. Can you go back and find them all?

Here's the paragraph again, with the commands marked in italics.

Sometimes, people ask me where you can *buy another copy of The Pitching Bible*, and I tell them that it's easy, you just *go into any book shop and ask*. You *see, for yourself*, one copy is often not enough and *it's good to have one* to make notes in and another to *enjoy it* as much as *you want to, tell all your friends*, and *enjoy it* together.

You might mark a command with a slight change in emphasis, or you might pause slightly before and after the command.

If you look back to the example at the start of this section, the

_____

7   Because a third party is saying the command, this also takes on the
     form of a story, making it even more influential

command is as follows:

"I was a bit nervous this morning but my friend told me to just *relax and enjoy my pitch*, so I'll do my best"

Remember, the more subtle the better. You should probably practice this on your friends before you use it in a pitch. It's a good idea to tell your friends that you're doing it so that they can give you feedback, rather than just thinking that you're being strange.

Negative Commands

I'm not saying that this book has all the answers for you, because I don't know what all of your questions are. To say that I can tell you how to pitch better in every situation is ridiculous, because I don't know what situations you are pitching in. So I would never suggest that you need to pay attention to every subtle point in this book, because I know there's so much to take in. So don't read this book over and over. Don't write sticky notes and mark out the pages that are most important. Don't make a list of the points that you're going to put into practice as you design your next pitch. And I'm certainly not going to tell you to visit The Pitch Doctor website and download the checklists to use.

Language has a few peculiarities that aren't present in your sensory experience. Can you remember the last time that you walked down the street and didn't see a lamp post? What about a computer keyboard? Can you remember the last time that you didn't see one?

Language can represent zeroes, negatives and opposites, but in the real world, there are no zeroes, negatives or opposites. In the real world, things can only exist. They can only ever not exist as a result of a memory.

When you were very young, your entire world comprised only what was available to your senses. When your parents showed you a toy, you laughed. When they hid it behind a book, you were sad. The toy had disappeared! It had ceased to exist. When they took the toy out and said, "Boo!", your excitement was overwhelming. The toy is back!

An important developmental test for children is to hide the toy and see if they look for it. If they look for it, they have reached the stage where they form mental maps of their world. Crucially, they know that the toy still exists, even though they can't see it any more.

Not long ago, someone gave me directions by saying that their house was opposite where the garage used to be. I'd never been there before, neither when there was a garage there nor after it had gone.

What is the opposite of red? It could be green, violet, wrote or unread. An opposite is only possible when you have a context. Red on a traffic light has a different meaning to red on a bunch of roses.

I can say:

□ Don't tell all your friends to buy The Pitching Bible

□ Tell none of your friends to buy The Pitching Bible

□ Tell your friends to buy a book; anything but The Pitching Bible

At first glance, you might think that I don't want you to tell your friends to buy The Pitching Bible, but when you consider what has to happen inside your mind in order to think about not telling your friends to buy The Pitching Bible, you first have to think about telling your friends to buy The Pitching Bible, so what has actually happened is that you have imagined telling your friends about The Pitching Bible, which is a good thing. No publicity is bad publicity.

Now

When my son Sam was five years old, I was walking in the park with him and he said to me, "Daddy, when would be a good time to buy me an ice cream now?"

The structure of his sentence made me think:

1. I've created a linguistic monster!

2. I am so proud

3. This is going to cost me a lot of money over the next twenty years!

The word 'now' has a special meaning. Each of us has a very different, unique and subjective concept of time. For some of us it passes quickly, for others, more slowly. Some of us see time as a series of impending deadlines, others see it as a range of possible paths ahead of us. And each of us has a different interpretation of the duration of "now".

5.6 Where is Now?

Imagine that you can see the flow of time as a visible line, like a project plan for your whole life, showing past, present and future.

Where is the past? Behind you, to the side or somewhere else?

Where is the future? Is it in front of you, to the side of you or somewhere else?

Where is now?

How big is now? (Indicate with your hands)

How long is now? (As in seconds, minutes, hours etc.)

Ask your friends, colleagues and family to answer these questions and note how they 'see' time.

Think about the differences between you and other people.

Do these differences explain any confusion or conflict that you have ever experienced relating to time, such as deadlines, priorities or a sense of urgency?

When you get to know your clients, you might notice that they too have different subjective experiences of time. This makes a huge difference when you are trying to keep control of the sales process and move things along at the right pace. If you feel that the client is taking too long to respond, they might be putting you off, or they might just have a very different understanding of what "soon" means.

Time is not a real entity, it is something that is only implied through movement and change in the world. We cannot sense time directly, we can only infer its passage indirectly with tools such as clocks and egg timers. Constants such as the force of gravity and the size of the grains of sand mean that the egg timer fills in around five minutes, every time.

Similarly, constants such as your client's business environment and their own sense of priority create a 'pace' for any project that you deliver with them.

Years ago, a business process required the manual typing of order forms, the distribution of internal memos, paperwork going backwards and forwards in the mail for signature, manual filing in filing rooms and it required all the people involved to be in the same place, every day.

Today, the majority of business processes are entirely automated. A manager types his or her emails, they arrive almost instantly and the sender expects an instant reply. Copies are made automatically, electronic signatures are acceptable and all of this can happen when the people involved are in the office, at home, on a train or, sadly, on holiday.

The pace of business life is largely dictated by technology. We generally want things done 'as soon as possible', whether that means two weeks or two seconds. Technology simply raises our expectations.

When you take some time to understand how your client perceives time, you can begin to influence the pace of the relationship.

An important aspect of time is expectation. Generally, people don't mind if something takes you an hour, or a week, just as long as they can plan in advance. If you say that you'll get something done 'right away' and it takes you until tomorrow, have you met the expectation that you set?

If you say that something will take you an hour and it takes you less than an hour, what do you do? Do you get back to the client and surprise them, or do you wait until the hour is up because you don't want to raise their expectations for future requests?

5.7 How Soon is Soon?

What period of time do these words imply to you?

Now	Soon	A moment
Currently	Recently	Right away
Imminent	ASAP	Immediate
Not long	A minute	Eventually
Not long ago	Ages	A while
A bit	Forever	A tick
Five minutes	A second	Back then

Ask your friends, family and colleagues to answer the questions too. What differences do you notice? How is that interesting?

What will you do differently when someone says they'll call you back "in five minutes" or when a client says they will review your proposal, "soon"?

Perhaps you might ask for a specific date and time?

My friend Jeremy Wilson, who is a project manager and recognised expert in large scale IT projects says, "Project managers often 'sand bag' or pad their timescales and deadlines. In turn, the people who are working on their projects do the same. Everyone builds in a little leeway in case everyone else fails to deliver on time. The result is that the project is delivered late, because no-one is working to an accurate expectation".

Giving and expecting clear timescales means that you can plan effectively and deliver against your promises, and it's meeting expectations that is important, not doing things quickly.

I often find that, when I ask someone when they can do something for me, they say, "I'll get back to you as soon as I can". I don't need it as soon as possible, I just need to know when it will be. If it's five minutes, make it five minutes. If it's a week, I can put a note in my diary.

Overall, if you focus on building high quality relationships and communicate your needs and intentions clearly, you're already way ahead of your competitors.

Aside from setting realistic expectations, how is a knowledge of the client's sense of time valuable when pitching?

Firstly, by bringing your pitch into the client's 'now' you increase their sense of urgency.

Consider a decision that you need to make. How do you feel differently about the following?

- ☐ You need to decide soon
- ☐ You need to decide imminently
- ☐ You need to decide at some point
- ☐ You need to decide right away
- ☐ You need to decide now
- ☐ You need to decide as a matter or urgency

Back in Secret Four we talked about the way that people use spatial location as a means of coding information, for example putting important tasks on the right of their desk or putting urgent tasks 'under their noses'.

Think about the conversations you had with people while you were trying out Exercise 5.6. If you haven't done it yet then go back, do not collect $200 and don't roll the dice again until you've finished it.

If you don't know how to find out where someone places 'now', how can you move your pitch into their awareness and make it their higher priority?

When you understand what your client means by 'now', you can design your slides, write your proposal and present your pitch so that the client feels an inexplicable sense of urgency around making a decision. And, after all, if your pitch is important enough for them to spend time paying attention to you, it's important enough to act upon right away, isn't it? This doesn't mean the client will automatically say 'yes', it means that the client is more likely to say 'yes' or 'no', sooner rather than later. The sooner you get a definitive response, the sooner you can get on with something more useful than chasing a decision.

Put it in Writing

Whilst a written proposal is sometimes the only way to get your pitch in front of the client, a written summary should always be part of your pitch.

There are a number of ways that you can structure a written proposal, and you can apply the same principles as for designing any other type of pitch.

The one important thing to remember about a written pitch is that you're not in control of the reader's attention, so you have to get your message across as quickly and succinctly as possible.

The usual way to do this is to put the summary first. You'll often see this as an 'executive summary' or a 'management summary', however it should be aimed at any reader, because anyone who takes the time to read your proposal is a potential decision maker or influencer.

A good newspaper story follows a fairly consistent format. The headline and the first paragraph answer the questions what, where, when, who, how and why.

However, the headline and first paragraph do not tell the whole story.

The purpose of the headline is to grab the reader's attention and make them want to read the first line. The purpose of the first line is to make the reader want to read the first paragraph, and the purpose of the first paragraph is to make the reader want to read the whole story.

Another way of looking at this is as a sales qualification process.

The purpose of the headline is to let potential readers know if the story will appeal to them or not.

For example, the headline, "Man Bites Dog" will get most peoples' attention, whereas the headline, "Lithuania in Tense Penalty Shootout" would probably appeal to a narrower audience, unless you happen to be a devoted supporter of Lithuania's national football team. The headline allows some readers to opt out, saving them time and allowing the writer to target the story to a specific group of readers.

Of course, discovering that the headline refers to a gun battle between the police and 'Jimmy Lithuania', the notorious gangster, over a parking ticket, might make the story interesting again.

The purpose of a news story is, ideally, to inform the reader. Some media also aim to influence the reader's opinion, perhaps towards in a particular political direction.

Therefore, one newspaper might carry a story on its front page about 15,000 patients not receiving the healthcare they need, whereas another newspaper might carry the same story on page ten, reporting that 2% of patients have to wait for operations. 2% doesn't sound too bad, whereas we recognise 15,000 as a big number. The first newspaper wants its readers to be outraged, the second wants its readers to think that healthcare standards are just fine.

If we take the idea of influencing the reader a stage further, we reach the world of advertising. An advertisement blatantly influences the reader, and also tells the reader what to do next. This final instruction is called a 'call to action'. The call to action instructs the reader to phone now, send in the reply card, visit any good book store or subscribe to a no obligation, limited edition, special discount, exclusive, once in a lifetime opportunity to acquire the product or service in question.

Let's put all this together and apply it to a written proposal.

Headline

Your proposal needs a headline, something to make the reader want to read further.

You can achieve this, firstly with a title for your proposal and secondly with a summary. In a proposal, the summary comes at the beginning and answers the question, "Why am I reading this?"

The summary should be between half a page and a page in length and should address the main points of the proposal.

The summary should be aimed directly at the decision maker, so if that person is a CEO, the summary will focus on return on investment and other business benefits. If the decision maker is a technical manager, the focus might be on cost of ownership, ease of management and other ways of making the manager's job easier or their team more effective.

In a business driven by budgets and business plans, every manager will be looking for ways to achieve more with their budgets. They'll be looking for ways to reduce headcount or increase productivity, and the more that you can help them to build their business case, the more aligned they will be with your proposal.

If you're pitching to non-profit organisations, it's easy to think that their motives and needs are completely different to those of banks and engineering companies. Whilst it is important to appeal to the ethics of a charity of public sector organisation, their budget constraints are as tight as those in the commercial sector if not tighter.

The summary needs to address all of the decision maker's primary decision criteria and leave them asking the question that will be answered by the rest of the proposal.

That question is, "but *how*?"

Six Questions

Your proposal needs to answer, in detail, the questions that the reader will have before they can make a decision.

Why

What is the reason for the proposal?

Are you addressing an identified business need, or is this a speculative proposal?

Why should the reader consider your proposal?

Why should the reader read more?

What

What are you proposing?

What are you asking for?

What are you offering in return?

What is your solution to the reader's business problem?

What will your proposal do for the reader?

How

How does your solution address the reader's needs?

How does your solution work?

Where

Where is the solution to be delivered?

When

When can the solution be delivered?

When does the client need to make a decision?

When does the client need to place an order?

Who

Who will be delivering the solution?

What does the client need to know about you and your company?

Call to Action

Your proposal needs to tell the reader what to do next.

The next step might be a meeting, an appointment with a designer, the supply of information or an order form. Remember, if you're not asking for something then you're not writing a proposal.

Purpose

The final point to bear in mind about a written proposal is its length. It should not be a word longer than is necessary to get the reader to make a decision.

If that means that your entire proposal is only one page long then that's good. Many sales people write proposals that are simply too long. At best, they waste their time writing too much and at worst, they switch the reader off and lose the business.

The purpose of the proposal is to give the reader the information necessary for a decision. If you need to educate the reader, the proposal is not the place to do it. You might go into sufficient detail about your technology, for example, to put the proposal into its proper perspective, but you should not be introducing anything new into the proposal that the client doesn't already know about.

Remember Secret One – the proposal is for the client's benefit, not yours.

Speak Your Mind

Your true feelings and intentions show up in your language, whether you like it or not. When you feel half hearted about something you try, and maybe, and should and ought.

If you think back to the 'Features and Benefits' section, you might realise that saying 'Features mean Benefits' or 'Benefits because Features' is very similar to saying 'Information means Meaning' or 'Meaning because Information'. If you give the audience the information first, they will use their own personal frame of reference to understand the meaning of that information, and that puts your pitch at the mercy of their preconceptions.

If you want the audience to make the right decision and take action, it is meaning that will motivate them, not information. Information never motivated anyone. Meaning caused dynasties and empires to rise and fall. Meaning built nations and moved mountains. Meaning is the reason why we do what we do, and your audience's search for meaning must be the start of your pitch, not the end of it.

Don't waste time trying to get every word right. Use the principles in this Secret, and this book, to get your goals and intentions right, and practice some of these linguistic tools to give your pitch the extra edge. If you try to follow a script that isn't coming from your heart, your audience will most definitely know about it.

By all means, mind your language, as long as you also remember to speak your mind.

Secret Brief

The Language of Pitching

Words are a sparse way to communicate your rich, vivid ideas into the client's mind. However, it's rather limiting to pitch without them. You need to understand how to use them to your fullest advantage.

Features and Benefits

Remember, it's benefits because features. Convey meaning first, then the information to support it.

WIIFM?

Get past the audience's 'WIIFM?' filter before they can listen to you

Questions

Questions don't convey information, do they?

Questions bypass the 'WIIFM?' filter and encourage interactivity.

Stories

I once met a man who told stories during his pitches, and they engaged and enthralled the audience like nothing else I've seen.

The Elevator Pitch

The Elevator Pitch is a trailer for the real thing. Don't try to cram everything into as short a time as possible, use any brief opportunity to move to the next stage; a pitch, not a purchase.

You Know How...

We can learn a few tips from comedians. Familiar experiences draw people together and the rules of improvisation help to build rapport.

Comedians use these techniques to get laughs. You can use them to win your pitch.

Getting a Feel for Language

Subtleties of language reveal how a person prefers to think, so if you present information to them in their preferred way, you make it easier for them to absorb and understand it.

Vaguely Specific

Hypnotists often have a bad image, especially where influence and persuasion are concerned. However, they do know a thing or two about communication, and there are a few tips that we can learn from them.

Commands

Often, the easiest way to get someone to do something is to tell them to do it. And if that doesn't work, just ask nicely.

Now

What do you want? And when do you want it?

Now is a rather vague period of time, and it's worth understanding what it really means.

Put it in Writing

Follow the same principles for a written pitch as you would for a face to face pitch.

Speak Your Mind

Whilst language is definitely important, don't try to script every word. Know what your outcome is, understand your pitch inside out and speak from your heart.

SECRET 6

SAY IT AGAIN SAM

Cover design concept by Sam Boross, age 9

Make it Memorable

Apparently, Humphrey Bogart never actually said, "Play it again, Sam" in the film Casablanca. Similarly, Captain Kirk never actually said, "Beam me up, Scotty". Our memories have become corrupted by nostalgia.

No matter how well we think we remember an event, we can always get a contradictory account from someone else who was there. Since each person interprets the event through their own senses, and each person's senses are filtered according to their own experiences, beliefs and expectations, we shouldn't be surprised when each person's memory of the event is different.

Therefore, one of the things that excellent pitchers do is to make sure that their message is getting across, exactly as they intended it to.

No doubt you have heard (perhaps earlier in this book?) the old presenter's adage, "Tell them what you're going to tell them, tell them, then tell them again".

It's easy to overlook these pearls of wisdom, so I will.

On second thoughts, let's have a closer look.

Firstly, read anything about the subject of 'Accelerated Learning' or about super memory techniques and one of the key principles is repetition. Remember that. Repetition. What's one of the key principles? Exactly right. Well done.

Secondly, tell them, tell them and tell them again. Three times. Listen to the speeches of Presidents and Prime Ministers. Their key points come in groups of three. Why is that? Well, we don't really know why, but we do know that it works. For some reason, groups of three sound good and they're easy to remember.

Groups of three are:

- ☐ Enjoyable

- ☐ Memorable

- ☐ Convincing

I once advised an advertising agency on an important pitch where the clients were coming to their offices. We arranged to have a certain piece of music playing, quietly, as they came into reception and throughout the presentation which reinforced the message of the presentation. We even got the driver to play it, softly, as he took them back to their offices. They won the pitch.

The important point for you to note here is consistency. If you want to reinforce your message, do things consistently. If you want to confuse your message, do things inconsistently.

Of course, straight repetition can be... well, repetitive.

The Nobel prize winning physicist Richard Fenyman lectured in South America and found that all of the University students there could recite all of the theories that they had learned, word for word. They were amongst the highest achieving students that Feynman had found, anywhere in the world. Yet when he posed them real world questions, as opposed to purely theoretical questions, he found that they didn't understand a single thing about physics.

Therefore, we need to understand a little more about how people learn in order to understand how we can use the concepts of repetition and consistency in more subtle and powerful ways.

Memories are Made of This

Do you remember this?

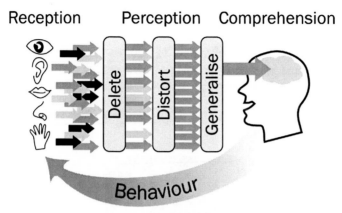

Reception   Perception   Comprehension

Delete   Distort   Generalise

Behaviour

Your memories are stored in the form of sensory data and shaped by your perceptual filters. Earlier, we talked about how to get information past those sensory filters in a number of ways, for example with stories and questions, or by using language that appeals to the client's communication preferences.

Therefore, an important way to make your pitch memorable and influential is to tune it to your audience, just like you would tune a radio to a radio station, otherwise all you hear is background static.

One of the important things to understand about your senses and therefore the process of learning is that your senses are differential. They are sensitive, not to the level of a stimulus but to a change in the level of that stimulus.

If you have a cat, you might have noticed it wake up when it hears a noise and go back to sleep as the noise continues. When the noise stops, it wakes up again.

6.1 Spot the Difference

Place your left hand, palm down, on a table top or similar surface. Carefully press the tip of your right index finger against the back of your left hand. Be sure to hold your hands very still. How long is it before you no longer feel the pressure?

The next time you watch television, fix your eyes on the centre of the screen and hold your gaze as still as you possibly can. What begins to happen after a few seconds?

Stare at the + in this image for thirty seconds, then look at a white surface. What do you see?

What does this tell you about how to make your pitch stand out from the background noise?

Our senses are designed for new experiences, for novelty. Our perceptions, which follow our senses, are designed for novelty. Our memories, which reflect our perceptions, are designed for novelty. We remember our first times, and we remember intense experiences more clearly than everyday experiences.

When Albert Einstein died in 1955, doctors wanted to examine his brain, thinking that it would be markedly bigger than the average human brain. In fact, they found that it was no different, structurally, to any other typical human brain.

Since then, with developments in neurology and brain analysis techniques, doctors have discovered that his brain is different, but not in ways that had been thought to be significant.

Most peoples' brains contain about the same number of cells. Our brains are all about the same size as each other. What varies is the number of connections between those cells.

More connections means that more information can be processed, and it seems that information is stored and processed throughout the brain, rather than in specialised locations.

Therefore, anything that encourages the creation of more connections is very important and very valuable.

You may have heard that a buyer needs to be exposed to a marketing message six or seven times before they will make a buying decision. You may have also heard that a buyer needs to receive six or seven sales calls before they will make a buying decision. Can this be a coincidence? If you want a client to remember you and your product or service, you might send them a brochure or place an advert and hope that the right people will read it.

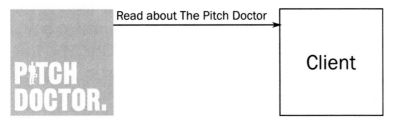

When someone reads about you, if they're interested, a weak connection will be formed. If they don't act upon it, that connection will fade away very quickly like a short term memory.

If you can make multiple connections, the link between you and the client gets stronger. Reinforcing one connection has some value, for example if the client reads the same advert every month in the same magazine, but reinforcing the overall connection in different ways is far more powerful.

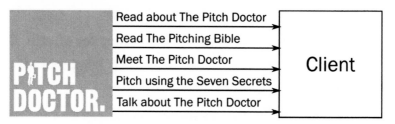

Do you remember this?

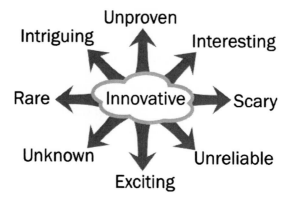

Each of these words is a label, used to recover a memory. Imagine that, in your brain, you have a bucket full of memories. Each memory can be pulled out of the bucket and experienced by pulling on the appropriate string. The label lets you know what kind of memory it is, and the more labels that are attached to a memory, the easier it is to pull out.

We could say that the more labels a memory has, the stronger it is.

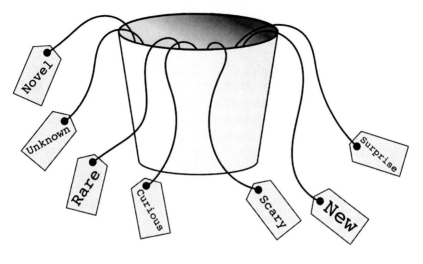

All of these labels are attached to the same memory; they are synonyms. You can take any of the strings and pull out the same memory.

What about memories that have very different labels?

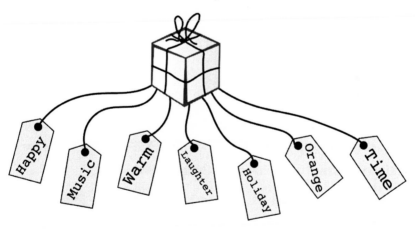

6.2 Memory labels

I'm going to give you a series of labels for memories. Each will bring a memory to mind. I want you to work though the list, one by one, starting with the first memory that comes to mind. If you can, stay with the same memory and explore deeper within it. If not, take the next memory that comes to mind. Just see where it takes you.

A childhood memory

The colour red

A boy's name beginning with R

A gift

A feeling

What memories are evoked by these words?

What does that mean?

We make new memories by connecting new experiences to what we already know. We make sense of new experiences by comparing them to our memories.

I'm sure you've heard people say, "Oh, it's just like..."

When you introduce a new idea in your pitch, no matter how innovative or revolutionary it is, your audience can only make sense of it by comparing it to what they already know.

Perhaps you have read the pretentious descriptions found in CD booklets; "Kris' music cannot be labelled or categorised, it is in a genre of its own with no familiar frame of reference or dusty, faded signpost to warn the listener about what to expect from this avant-garde, renaissance virtuoso. Some have called him a musician, others a performer, but these do not sum up the depth of his rare and unique, timeless, nameless talent. His fans call him Kris, we call him a legend in the making."

Do you want your audience to categorise your pitch? Of course not, because that puts the audience in control, and it undoes the hard work you have done in conveying your dream into their minds.

By connecting concepts and ideas together, by creating a chain or a journey, you create a series of foundations that lead the audience towards an outcome that is far more under your control.

Learning Styles

David Kolb published his learning styles model in 1984 as Kolb's experiential learning theory (ELT).

The idea behind this model is quite straightforward once you see that it represents a cycle of learning with four stages, which relate to either taking in new information or analysing it. Let's say you want to learn how to tie a knot. You can watch someone else do it or have a go yourself, and you can either analyse the real experience you had, or you can form an abstract theory.

Onto Kolb's four learning stages, Peter Honey and Alan Mumford mapped the four roles shown in the diagram; Activist, Pragmatist, Theorist and Reflector. For example, a Pragmatist prefers to think first and then do, whereas a Theorist prefers to observe an activity and then think about it in order to form a theory.

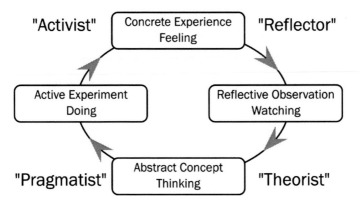

Do you see the relevance of this to the success of your pitch?

In order for the audience to make a decision, they need information. Another word that we use to describe the taking in of information is learning. Therefore, the audience for your pitch needs to learn about your idea in order to form an opinion about it and thereby make a decision.

In Kolb's model, there are four learning stages; Think, Do, Feel and Watch.

How many of those stages are present in your pitch? Typically, the audience will be Watching and Thinking. The ideal person to respond to that will be a 'Theorist'. Theorists like to observe and then draw conclusions from what they have observed.

I hope that by now, you're spotting a problem.

Potentially, three quarters of the audience don't learn that way.

Here's another problem for you.

The people that do happen to learn that way need time to reflect. Therefore, trying to cram more information into them will not make them learn any more. If they don't have time to step back, mentally, and sort through the new information they've received, their brains get full and they stop listening.

As a pitcher, you might not have thought of yourself as a teacher, but the principles are the same. If you want the audience to make a decision in your favour, they need to remember and understand what you have told them, which means that they have learned it.

What can you do to help the audience to learn more easily?

Let's have a look at how the different learning styles work.

Activist

Activists need to do something and they learn by experimenting. If you can get the audience to do something during the pitch, the activists get what they need. Perhaps they can try out a product sample or take part in a demonstration. Importantly, they need to experience something for themselves and work out how they feel about it, so they make decisions based on their instincts more than on logic. Activists seek hands on experience and get bored with implementation.

Activists say, "Can I have a go?"

Pragmatist

Pragmatists like to do what works. They like to have a theory first and then see if they can put it into practice. They like puzzles, because they like to think up the solution first and then try it out. They need to take part, like the activists, but they need an idea about what to do, whereas the activists like to dive in head first. Pragmatists like to find practical applications for ideas and get bored with long theoretical discussions.

Pragmatists say, "Does it work?"

Theorist

Theorists like to observe what's going on and then form a theory or opinion about it. While the activists and pragmatists are busy entertaining themselves, the theorists are figuring out the rules. Theorists like evidence, logical explanations, facts and figures. They don't like subjectivity and exaggeration.

Theorists say, "How does it work?"

Reflector

Reflectors like to observe and reflect and turn things around from different points of view. They like to use their imagination to solve problems rather than diving in like the activists. They like to take time to ponder and don't rush into decisions until they think that they have covered all the angles.

Reflectors say, "Let me think about it."

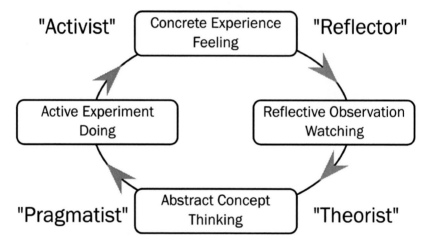

People are not fixed in these roles, they are preferences. We all need time to reflect, we all need to take part, we all need to create rules and we all need experience to confirm those rules. You could therefore think of the roles above as a bias towards a particular learning sequence.

How do you think you can design your pitch so that it caters for these different learning styles?

Simply, try to include things for the audience to do and watch, and give them opportunities to think and feel.

Style	How to incorporate...
Watch	Pitch!
Do	Join in, demonstrate, try samples
Think	Facts, research, structure
Feel	Comment on their reactions and instincts

In general, Theorists and Pragmatists are more biased towards rules or abstract concepts, so they can tend to have more obvious preconceptions. Reflectors and Activists are more biased towards new experiences, so can appear to be more open minded.

Remember that learning is not a static event; it requires movement. Learning, and therefore the process of deciding, requires Experience, Observation, Thinking and Doing. Make sure that you build something into your pitch that takes your audience through this sequence, either in some physical sense or in language.

You're probably looking for a real example of this in action. The fact that you are is a perfect example of this process. Before you can understand, you need to either have or be able to relate to some kind of concrete experience, so I'll talk you through a couple of scenarios so that you can see what you think, imagine trying it out for yourself and get to grips with how valuable it can be for you.

That was the first example...

Here's another. If your product lends itself to a physical demonstration, you can pitch your product, give the audience the opportunity to discuss it amongst themselves, ask them what they would like to try out for themselves, let them have a go, give them time to reflect on the experience, get them to discuss their experience and get them to work out how best to use or sell the product.

If you're in the UK, I suggest you watch the TV program 'Dragon's Den'. If you're not in the UK, look it up and watch it online.

The US version of the show, American Inventor, seems to be less varied in its pitch format, so do look out for the UK version.

The program follows a similar format each week. Prospective entrepreneurs pitch their business idea to five investors. If the investors think that they can turn the idea into a viable, profitable business, they offer cash in return for a share in the business.

Some pitches fail because the 'Dragons' don't see how the product can make money. Some fail because the price demanded by the entrepreneur is too high. Some fail because the Dragons take a dislike to the entrepreneur.

When you watch the program, you'll soon discover that the Dragons behave rather predictably. They want the entrepreneur's numbers to add up, and they want the entrepreneurs to listen to the Dragons' advice. That's not to say that the Dragons are experts in the product; they're testing to see if they can work with the entrepreneur, to find out if the entrepreneur is open to their advice and input. If they're not, it doesn't matter how good the idea is, the Dragons know that the working relationship will be too difficult and therefore too time consuming. The Dragons want their money to do most of the work.

The pitches that I'm suggesting you watch out for are the ones where the idea is interesting, but not a guaranteed winner, and the Dragons' attention is on the entrepreneur. There is something about the person that makes them worth the investment, even if the idea itself needs a bit of work.

Of all the examples that I've seen, the successful pitch has a combination of the 'learning cycle' stages that we have been discussing. The Dragons don't know why they feel positive towards an idea, and on paper it might not completely stack up, but, somehow, they feel that the entrepreneur is worth the investment.

This encapsulates the very essence of what I'm aiming to get across to you in this book. Some pitches are – or should be – a guaranteed win for you. The product is right, the relationship is right, the commercial framework is right and the pitch itself is a formality.

Some pitches are a guaranteed loss. You know that you're way out on price, you know that you are just making up the numbers, you know that you're only there so that the client can go through the motions of making a 'fair' decision. You knew it, but you went along anyway, just in case. You thought that, rather than focus your resources on something more worthwhile, you'd have a go. You really should have qualified out some time ago, or you were never close enough to the deal to realise that you should have qualified out. Or you've spent so long chasing the client that you can't admit to your manager that it was all a waste of time.

What we need to concentrate on is the pitches that could go either way, and the deciding factor is the quality of your pitch.

Here's a diagram that you may have seen before, perhaps at school when you were learning about statistics.

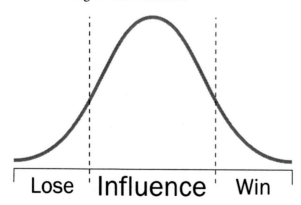

Having a father who is a retired economist, I know that the important thing to remember about statistics is that they are not predictions – they are measurements of what has already happened.

This diagram is sometimes called a 'bell curve' or to give it its technically correct name, a 'normal distribution curve'. The normal distribution is related to the 80/20 rule that you are no doubt familiar with. 80% of your customers generate 20% of your revenue, 20% of your customers cause 80% of your problems, and so on.

Lots of people get hung up on the 80/20 figure, but you really don't have to worry about it. It's a quirk of the statistics. If you take the middle 20% of the curve, you'll find that the area underneath it is 80% of the total area of the graph.

Some people mistrust statistics, quoting Mark Twain, Benjamin Disraeli and Charles Wentworth Dilke who all said that there are, "lies, damned lies and statistics". Certainly, some people have been known to use statistics to misrepresent facts. Financial misreporting scandals often start by hiding small problems with statistics.

The most common problem with statistics is that people use them to try to predict the future. Statistics can tell us what is more *likely* to happen, but they cannot tell us what *will* happen.

What the statistics cannot tell you is whether a prospective client will fall into the 80% or the 20%. The statistics cannot tell you whether you will win or lose a particular pitch. The statistics can only tell you that you will lose one in every five pitches. Knowing last week's lottery numbers does not help you to predict this week's draw. If you flip a coin and get 9 heads in a row, the next flip is no more likely to result in a tail than another head.

Statistics are often counter intuitive, because humans like to look for patterns in the world. If you lose four pitches in a row, it's not a run of bad luck. There is something that you are systematically doing wrong. You have to find that error and eliminate it - and be prepared to leave no stone unturned.

Remember, you will lose some pitches simply because you are not operating in a monopoly. If you were, you wouldn't have to pitch. The very nature of pitching is competitive, and clients will not always make decisions for the reasons that you think they should.

When you look back at all of the pitches you have ever delivered, you will find that about 20% were won from the start and you went on to win them. You will also find that about 20% were lost from the start and you went on to lose them.

That leaves 60% of pitches - three out of five - where the outcome was based on the pitch itself.

Breaking that down further, there are situations where the effectiveness of your pitch turned a potential loss into a win. These account for 20% of the 60% that you influenced.

Equally, there are situations where the business was yours and you made such a mess of the pitch that the client just couldn't make the decision in your favour. These also account for 20% of the 60% that you influenced.

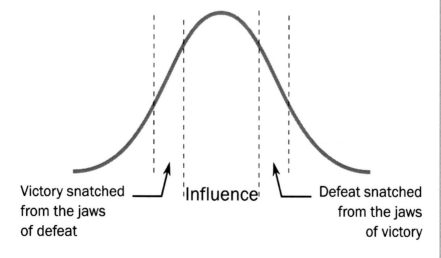

Victory snatched from the jaws of defeat · Influence · Defeat snatched from the jaws of victory

That leaves a total of 36% of all pitches where the sole deciding factor is the effectiveness of your pitch. That's just over a third.

Again, this isn't a prediction, and it's not something you can influence. You can't change the laws of physics, or in this case, statistics. Review your own pitches and see for yourself.

So what can you do? All other things being equal, this means that you could win 80% of all pitches that you are invited to deliver. By ruthlessly qualifying out the ones that are a definite loss, you focus more of your precious time on the ones that you can influence, and you make sure that you don't get complacent about the ones that are yours to win.

Just because a pitch is in your 'win' column doesn't mean that it's in your competitors' 'lose' columns. For one of them, it could be a pitch that they could influence. Regardless of how confident you feel, you have to treat every pitch as if you could lose it.

Again, look at your own statistics. One in every five pitches that you deliver is won simply because you turn up. One in every five is lost regardless of what you do. What happened with the other three?

Unfortunately, you are likely to lose at least one in five pitches, regardless of what you do and how much you improve your skills. These pitches are opportunities to learn. If you only pitch when you know that a win is guaranteed, you'll learn nothing.

If you play a sport against someone who you know you can always beat easily, you'll never improve. In fact, your game will deteriorate to the level where you're only slightly better than your opponent. Improving your game means that you have to play a lot of opponents who will beat you. The more you lose, the better you get, unless you attribute losing to factors outside of your control, or if your opponents have such a significant physical advantage that you really have no chance anyway. If your opponents always have better equipment or better luck, you'll never improve your game.

The more competitive you and your opponents are, the more you will each improvise and try new tactics. No doubt you've seen this in your business, where your competitors have tried different approaches to pitching.

Some of these new approaches 'work', in that the clients like them and are influenced by them, whereas some of them 'don't work' in that they make no difference or, worse, have a negative effect.

The criteria for a tactic 'working' is that it wins the pitch. When people indiscriminately change what they do in each pitch, they are unable to measure the effectiveness of what they do. In order to know if a tactic 'works', you have to keep everything else the same and use the tactic several times before you can be sure that it's getting the result that you think it is.

For example, if you keep on losing at tennis and, one day, you decide to wear some new lucky shoes, use an expensive new racket, focus on serving to your opponent's weak side, focus on staying in the middle of the court, imagine your opponent being physically smaller than you, promise yourself a new car if you win and eat a bowl of strawberries before the game then you have no way of knowing which of these new tactics made the biggest difference.

Rationally, you can look at the list and guess that the service made the biggest difference. Unfortunately, the hapless player will tend to think that there was nothing wrong with his or her serve to begin with, therefore it must have been the lucky shoes. You'll recognise this superstitious approach as that of the Struggler.

In the introduction to this book, The Seven Secrets, I mentioned Darwin. You probably wondered back then why I used him as an example. It's important that you recognise that you are not playing in a static environment. As you learn and evolve, your opponents do too. As you improve your game, your opponents improve theirs.

When you're playing one to one with an opponent, there is a very short connection between your innovation and their response.

When you're playing indirectly through a third party such as a business market, evolution happens more slowly. Your competitors don't respond in real time because they find out indirectly about your innovations and successes. When they find that you are winning more pitches because you are using a famous actor to deliver them, they hire an actor too and your advantage is neutralised.

The rules of the game stay the same and the players get better at developing their own strengths while exploiting their opponents' weaknesses.

Let's say you're playing tennis against Alan and Bob. Alan has a weak backhand, so you always serve to his backhand. Bob isn't very agile, so you make him run around. When Alan comes back from Tennis camp and Bob comes back from physiotherapy, they have protected their weaknesses. Now the playing field is level, and you're at a disadvantage, because your one winning tactic no longer works. If you want to win, you have to improvise and adapt.

To discover why a competitor is winning more pitches than you are, you have to get real data and you have to analyse it objectively.

When you analyse, objectively, why your opponent beat you, you can adapt. There's no point copying what they do, because next time they'll do something different. They don't beat you because of a particular move or strategy – they beat you because they are better at exploiting your weaknesses than you are at exploiting theirs.

The competitors who beat you aren't better at pitching than you are – they are better at learning.

How does all of this relate to Secret Six?

Repetition is fundamental to learning, but that doesn't mean saying the same thing over and over again.

Whilst you may have learned your times tables at school by repetitive chanting, you're unlikely to get an audience to do that, although if you have a punchline or slogan, why not make a joke of getting the audience to repeat it?

In my 'Seven Secrets' lecture, I make a joke of the concept of repetition by getting the audience to join in. I say, "What's the key to learning?" and they all shout back "Repetition!". I say, "One more time!" and they shout "Repetition!" I show a slide of a teacher with "I must remember the Pitch Doctor" written several times on his blackboard. It may be a light hearted point, but the underlying value of it is that the audience are interacting, joining in and getting the message.

Demonstrators have simple slogans that anyone can join in with and chant. "What do we want?" and "When do we want it?" is one. The US Army's marching chants are another example; "I don't know but I've been told..."

Repetition, for our purposes, means passing the same message or information through as many of the audience's learning channels as possible.

For example, they can watch and listen to your pitch, write something down, read it, say it out loud, have a go at something, reflect on their experience, discuss it with others and go through that whole cycle as many times as possible.

Let's say that your pitch has an amazing fact in it. Let's say that you have done some market research and you have discovered that 98% of the population has no idea whether their hot tap is on the left or the right. Do you know?

So, you give the audience a pen and a piece of paper. Then you show them a tap. Then you ask them to write down whether the hot tap is on the left or the right, or which way the lever turns for hot.

Then you ask them to reveal their answers and work out the percentage of people who didn't know.

Then you reveal your amazing statistic.

After you have given them time to ponder on the dire implications of this fact, you show them your invention, or pitch your idea for a film, or whatever it is that you are showing them.

What you're actually doing is giving them the same statistic in a number of different ways. You're giving them a context within which to draw a conclusion. Without that, the fact itself is meaningless.

Saying that three out of five pitches can be influenced by you would also have been a meaningless fact if I hadn't illustrated it.

Stop for a moment and think about it. Even the language tells you what to do – illustrate a point. You draw a picture of it. If not on a whiteboard or proposal then directly into the client's mind using all of the sensory richness of your language. Wrap the audience in the comforting blanket of the sights, sounds, tastes, smells and feelings of a wonderfully confident decision.

Holding Attention

If you have ever looked out at an audience and wondered, "Why aren't they listening to me?", then you can feel reassured that the answer was that they can't, and it's not always your fault.

Another key to effective learning is holding the audience's attention. Do you remember AIDA? Get the audience's Attention, then hold their Interest?

One problem that faces pitchers is that the time allowed for a typical pitch is longer than most people can pay attention for.

During the pitch, the audience's attention naturally wanes. If the room is dark and the presenter's voice is a droning monotone, this process is greatly accelerated.

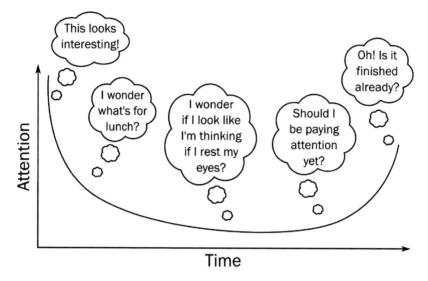

There are broadly two solutions to this problem; either make your pitch so short that you have the audience's attention throughout, or break the pitch into a number of shorter sections.

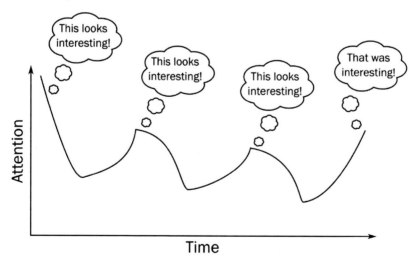

How can you recapture the audience's attention?

- You could reiterate what you said at the beginning of your pitch

- You could ask the audience a few questions, encouraging a short period of interactivity

- You could give the audience an interactive demonstration which builds up through a number of steps

- You could pause and give the audience time to reflect

Remember that people need time to reflect in order to process new information, so for the audience to really understand your pitch, especially if it's something that needs careful consideration or imagination, you need to give the audience time to reflect. You literally need to pause for thought.

The more you move the audience's attention 'inside' by asking them to use their imaginations, the more likely they are to drift into a daydream. Therefore, if you are going to invite the audience to imagine, you need to mark the end of that very distinctly by bringing the audience's attention back 'outside', to the room and to your pitch.

Remember too that interrupting the audience's daydream potentially breaks rapport, particularly if they were really enjoying it.

There isn't much point in carrying on regardless and trying to cram in as much as possible because time is short. The more information that you throw at the audience, the more time they need to reflect in order to absorb that information. Therefore, if you pitch faster than your audience can think, they will reach saturation point and will be unable to take in any more of your pitch, no matter how good your idea or product is.

Pitch Blindness

If the client has seen pitches from a number of suppliers, they will all begin to merge into one. By mid-morning, the client won't be able to remember who said what, to who, about what.

After the third potential supplier has dazzled the client with their ground breaking, innovative, exclusive, revolutionary, world class, industrial strength, no nonsense pitch, the client will be suffering from 'pitch blindness'.

The biggest threat to your pitch in this instance is that your pitch becomes part of the background noise, and shouting louder just makes the background noise louder.

When I was just eleven years old, two BBC Radio producers came to my school, looking for children to take part in a new magazine program which was the first on British radio to be presented by children for children.

With so many children wanting to be chosen, I instinctively knew that I had to stand out from the crowd, so I offered to help the producers with a problem that they had. The test reading was for a boy and a girl, and more boys than girls wanted to audition. I volunteered to read the girl's part for all of the remaining boys who didn't have a girl to read with, and, if I say so myself, played the part pretty well. Not only did I stand out, I also had multiple opportunities to 'pitch' to the producers.

I was one of the five children chosen from 120 auditions, and we recorded two series and a Christmas special, interviewing the biggest television and music stars of the day.

Now, I'm not suggesting that you cross dress in order to win your pitch. Just stand out from the crowd.

If I've Told You Once...

I've told you a thousand times. It really doesn't matter how many times you tell me, you have to tell me, show me, get me to tell you, write it down, try it out, play with it, hold it, use it, buy it and then I might have some idea of what you're talking about.

When you have communicated your dream into your client's mind, you have to make sure it doesn't slip out again before you reach the all important part – the part where the client takes action.

Secret Brief

Make it Memorable

I saw a really great pitch once. I can't remember what it was about or who the company was, but it was very enjoyable.

That makes it a terrible pitch.

How many adverts can you remember where you have no idea what the product is that they're advertising?

Memories are Made of This

If you can understand how memories are formed and stored, you have a better chance of influencing what people remember, which means you have a better chance of influencing their decisions.

Learning Styles

In order to make a decision, the audience must absorb, organise and understand new information. This is essentially the process of learning, so by understanding different learning styles, you can organise your pitch to be more effective.

Holding Attention

It's not always realistic to hold the audience's attention throughout your entire pitch, however there are a number of ways that you can make more of a typical audience's attention span.

Pitch Blindness

When a client has seen too many pitches, they become pitch blind and you risk becoming part of the background noise. By standing out, you greatly increase your chances of being memorable and of influencing the client's decision.

SECRET 7

THE END
...OR IS IT?

The End?

What do you do at the end of your pitch?

Do you make for the door as quickly as you can, relieved that it's finally over?

Do you hang around like the last person at the party, talking to all the stragglers?

Do you make a grand exit?

Or do you try to slip out without anyone noticing?

You need to put as much effort into what you do at the end of your pitch as you put into planning and preparing for the start of it.

Why?

Well, what was the last film you saw at the cinema?

What was the first film you saw at the cinema?

What was the tenth film you saw?

There are many reasons why the end of your pitch is important, and why you must not leave the lasting impression that your clients have to chance, and this is just one of them.

In Secret Six, we talked about some of the principles of accelerated learning, and one principle that we missed out was a principle called 'primacy and recency'.

In simple terms, we tend to remember the start and end of something more easily than we remember the middle. We remember the first instance of something and the most recent instance of it, and not much in between. This ties in with what we know about our senses; that they detect changes in information, not absolute levels. The first and last times we experience something mark a transition, and we are programmed to detect changes, or transitions, in the world around us.

How you begin and how you end your pitch are therefore potentially more important than what you say in the middle.

Now I'm not suggesting that you end with a song and dance routine, or fireworks, or some other grand finale, I'm just saying that your pitch has to have a clearly defined end. It cannot fizzle out when the audience has lost interest. The pitch must end when you say it ends.

Questions

When should you take questions?

What many people will do is to announce that their pitch has ended and then invite questions. They will literally say something like, "Thank you, that's the end of my pitch, do you have any questions?"

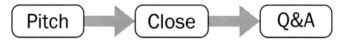

Have you ever said that?

The pitch is your pitch, right until the moment you walk out of the door. Why give it back to the audience prematurely?

When you close your pitch and then invite questions, you:

☐ Hand control back to the audience before you have finished

☐ Allow the audience to dictate the pace of the questions

☐ Allow the audience to decide when there are no more questions

☐ Allow the audience to decide when the pitch ends

☐ Miss the golden opportunity to incorporate the questions into your summary

If you close the presentation and then invite questions, you are telling the audience that you failed to cover everything they needed. Their perception will be that they got what they needed by asking you questions. The presentation fizzles out when there are no more questions or you run out of time.

What should you do instead?

Take questions before you close the pitch, of course. I'm sure you had already figured that out. It's simply a question of when and how.

The solution is very simple. Invite questions just before you are ready to summarise your pitch.

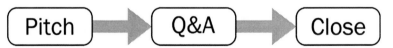

The important thing to remember is to tell the audience that you are allowing some time for questions before you close. If you say that your pitch has ended, you give control back. The result will most likely be that you'll never deliver your summary because the audience didn't know that you hadn't finished. They'll just think it odd that you didn't summarise.

Here's what you might say when taking questions at the end:

"Thank you for your time and attention, that concludes my pitch. Are there any questions?"

Here's an example of the right way to do it:

"At this point I'd like to allow ten minutes for questions before I close my pitch. What questions do you have?"

When you know exactly how long you are going to allow for questions, you can then decide whether each question has a short answer, in which case you can answer it, or a long answer, in which case you can offer a full discussion after your pitch. If you only have a few questions, you are in full control of moving on and bringing your pitch to an end sooner, which implies control and good organisation. If the questions are coming thick and fast then you can immediately offer a follow up meeting, because the audience's interest is their incentive to grant that opportunity.

If there are a lot of questions from the audience then the risk you are faced with is that your pitch turns into a discussion. The pitch is your time, your space and your opportunity to get your message across. If an interactive workshop turns out to be more appropriate then arrange that with the client as a follow up event, but don't let them drag your pitch from pillar to post because this means that you have allowed the audience to take control.

If you invite questions and then close the presentation with a summary that includes their questions, you are telling the audience that you are flexible and authoritative, and that you are adapting to their needs. Their perception will be that the presentation was interactive and that it gave them everything they needed. Remember primacy and recency. The presentation ends cleanly when you decide to close it.

Compare your pitch to a film. Does a film end, or does it just fizzle out when the characters have nothing left to say?

Why Do People Ask Questions?

It seems a bit pointless to ask, doesn't it? Why do people ask questions? Because they don't understand something. Because they want an answer. It's obvious.

Think about a typical presentation or meeting. Are the questions that people ask really what they seem to be?

Or do you sometimes wonder if there is some other motive behind the question?

Have you ever been asked a question while you were presenting and you just got the feeling that the person didn't really want the answer? Did you get drawn into a conversation, or did you feel that they were just trying to make a point?

In fact, when you think about it, the genuine questions were probably in the minority.

So, why do people ask questions?

- To demonstrate knowledge
- To demonstrate superiority over the presenter
- To disguise an objection
- To provoke a response from the presenter
- To provoke a response from another audience member
- To demonstrate attentiveness
- To waste time
- To set up for an attack
- To hide the fact that they weren't listening
- To gain control
- To learn something

Leading questions, or at least questions that are not motivated by an interest in the answer, can lead you away from your intended direction and prevent you from getting your message across.

Handling Questions

If you think back to what we talked about in Secret Five, Mind Your Language, you'll recall that questions are a very powerful communication tool which can bypass the audience's natural critical filtering process, their 'WIIFM?' filter.

If you haven't already realised it, questions can also bypass your filter too, can't they? When someone in the audience asks a question, it can stop an unprepared presenter in his or her tracks. The power of a question to focus the listener's attention works both ways.

You need to apply some discipline when handling questions, otherwise you run the risk of being sidetracked, and if you run out of time before you have put your message across, your pitch is doomed.

Whether you're going to take questions throughout the presentation or just before your summary, you need to do these things:

- Allow time in your schedule – as a rule of thumb, plan your pitch to last about three-quarters of your allocated time.

- Handle questions using the format that I'm going to give you in a moment, otherwise you will get sidetracked, which dilutes your key message and eats up time

- Preferably have someone else manage the Q&A process for you to prevent you from getting drawn in to the questions

- Make a note of the questions so that you can incorporate your answers into the end of your pitch

Whether you take questions in the middle or all at once in a dedicated Q&A section, you need to handle them in the same way, otherwise you hand control of the pitch back to the audience, and that is a very bad thing.

The solution to this is very simple:

☐ Pause

☐ Repeat the question

☐ Clarify the question

☐ Answer the question (if you want to)

This is a very important process to remember, so let's see if we can come up with a better way to remember it. In Secret Six, we learned about some of the principles of effective learning, so let's put them to good use.

What do you think might be a word that most presenters will say most often while they're presenting? Well it's not a word as such, but we'll pretend that it is.

The word is, "Err...."

Next, we'll think back to the exercises we've done around "anchoring", where you attached a feeling or state to a colour, word, music or perhaps a touch. Let's anchor something to the word 'Err'.

Remember Secret Six? Say It Again, Sam? Accelerated learning? Memory? Another valuable memory aid is the mnemonic.

Do you remember the colours of the spectrum? Richard Of York Gave Battle In Vain?

Let's make ERR a mnemonic. It's a bit of a squeeze but we'll do our best.

Here's the way it works.

Someone asks you a question.

You say, "Err..."

Echo

Rephrase

Reply

Remember that ERR means that you Echo back their question, then you Rephrase it to show you understand, then Reply if appropriate.

Why is this important? Why not just answer the question?

Firstly, it is genuinely useful to make sure you're answering the question you think you're answering, so you can check this by Echoing it back. When you Echo back the question, the questioner can decide if that's what they really meant to ask you.

When you Echo the question, use the questioner's words exactly.

Secondly, when you Rephrase the question, you give the questioner another chance to check that what you understand is what they meant. It also gives you a chance to check that the questioner's motives are genuine.

For example, someone might ask, "Is this going to be reliable?" Of course, you're going to say yes. They know you're going to say yes. Why would anyone expect you to say, "Actually, no, it's not very reliable but I still have a sales target to hit". What are they really saying? Are they saying that they're worried that your product will be unreliable? Possibly. Are they saying that your competitor has told them that your product is unreliable? Possibly.

So you might Rephrase the question with, "Are you asking for reliability figures, or would you find reports from reference customers more reassuring?"

In Rephrasing the question, you have appealed to their need either for reassurance or for raw data from which to draw their own conclusions.

Finally, you can Reply, but only if you want to. You may choose to defer the question until later, if it breaks the flow of your pitch, or you may ask the questioner to ask it again when you get to the Q&A part of your pitch. During your Q&A section itself, you generally would Reply unless the question led to a group discussion and you felt it wasn't necessary to join in. This would usually be the case when the questioner's colleagues do a better sales job than you could have done yourself!

The final accelerated learning trick that we can borrow is to mentally rehearse this a few times. Imagine that you're pitching, facing the audience. Someone asks a question and as you say, "Err..." you find yourself Echoing their question, Rephrasing it and Replying, if you want to.

When you have a number of people presenting with a panel Q&A session at the end, the approach is a little different.

In this situation, one person will have the role of managing the questions. Here's what they do:

1. Invite questions from the audience

2. Select someone to ask a question

3. Repeat the question so that the whole audience can hear it, and clarify it if necessary

4. Select a speaker to respond

5. Check that the answer is satisfactory

6. Move to the next person with a question or close the Q&A

You can see how steps 3 and 4 are partly designed to give the speaker time to think of a good answer!

When you're pitching in a team, one person manages the Q&A part of the pitch, leaving the rest of the team to handle questions and, importantly, record them for use in your follow-up.

When you're pitching by yourself, just remember to say "ERR".

Anticipating Questions

There will be certain questions that you can anticipate from the audience, so by addressing these in your pitch, you save time.

If you have been doing your homework about the audience, you might anticipate awkward questions, posed by someone who favours your competitor. There's nothing to be gained in avoiding awkward questions, because to be asked the question potentially puts the questioner in control.

By anticipating questions, you are in control of how and when you answer them.

Just Five More Minutes.... Pleeeeease

Some presenters use questions as a lazy way of closing their pitch. Rather than come up with something memorable, they say something like, "That's all I have to say, do you have any questions?", and the audience is then in control.

No matter how carefully you close your pitch, there's always a chance that someone in the audience will have saved their question for when they think you've finished. This might be because they've only just thought of it, or it might be because they want to upstage you.

It's a similar situation to when a child says, at bedtime, "Awww... just five more minutes, then I promise I'll go straight to sleep". The parent that gives in to this is still there, an hour later, trying to get a tired and over stimulated child to go to bed, which is like putting a cat into a basket prior to a visit the vet.

There is a small chance that the questioner really did just think of their question. There is a much greater chance that they have held on to the question for some time, waiting for you to finish so that they could pounce. And there is a very high chance that the question will be irrelevant in some way.

It's a difficult situation to be in when you have planned your pitch so methodically, so what you can bear in mind is that when you say the pitch has ended, you hand control of the room back to the audience. Therefore, any question that comes after that moment is not yours to deal with. Strictly speaking, the chairman needs to decide how to handle the question, so if you like, you can ask the host what he or she would like you to do; take a few more minutes outside of your pitch to answer extra questions, or respond 'offline' by email or telephone.

If they slip their question in just before you hand the room back, you could say, "I'm sorry, I've used all the time that you've given me for my pitch". If you don't then one more question can turn into one more, and one more, and one more. Five more minutes and then I really, really, really promise to go straight to sleep.

At this point the audience is left with the impression of a badly designed, badly delivered pitch that ran over time and didn't address all of the audience's questions. And after you've worked so hard to craft every detail of your pitch, you're not going to let the audience get away with that, are you?

You also have an opportunity to say, "If there are more questions, why don't we arrange another meeting, after we've all had time to reflect, so that we can discuss the way forward?" After all, if the audience is still thinking of more questions, they must be really interested. Why deny them the chance to hear more?

By marking out the time for questions, you maintain control of your pitch. Often, at least one person in the audience will try to wrestle that control back by asking questions outside of that time. The smaller the audience, the more disruptive this can be. Therefore, maintaining control might seem harsh when it's just one more question and, after all, what harm can it do? But when you're still standing there with your final slide up on the screen, twenty minutes after your pitch was supposed to end and you've been dragged into a conversation with one person while the rest of the audience shuffles and looks at their watches, you will wish you had dealt with it more firmly when you had the chance.

Closing Your Pitch

Closing your pitch means much more than simply saying 'thank you' and running for the door.

☐ The close serves three vital purposes:

☐ The close wraps up any loose ends from your pitch

☐ The close drives home your main message

The close marks the point where you hand the room back to the audience

☐ There are many ways that you can choose to close your pitch.

☐ You could end with a summary of the key message

☐ You could end with a call to action, as in the AIDA format

☐ You could end by repeating what you said at the beginning of the pitch

☐ You could end with reference to something that has been in the audience's view throughout your pitch, placed solely to engage their curiosity

☐ You could end by fulfilling a promise that you make at the start of your pitch

☐ You could end just by saying "thank you"

Closing your pitch is much more than just the end, the last slide, the punchline. It is part of the way that you mark out your territory and acknowledge that you have been granted that opportunity by your host.

We're not talking an Oscar acceptance speech... "I'd like to thank John for inviting me here today, and my Mother, and my therapist, and everyone who knows me..."

Think about a cabaret performance. Each act in the show is important. Without the supporting acts, there is nothing to build up to the headline act.

Cinemas used to show 'news reels' and cartoons before the 'feature presentation', whereas adverts and trailers have now taken their place. The effect is the same though; building up your anticipation and focusing your attention on the film.

Each act in the cabaret has an end; its own finale. The show itself builds up like a series of waves, leading to the grandest finale of all at the end of the show, at which point the house lights come on and the theatre belongs, once again, to the audience.

What you're doing by closing your pitch is acknowledging that the client has given you an audience, literally, for your pitch, and so your pitch resides within your relationship with your client, and that relationship resides within your business world.

Marking out your territory is important, and what is equally important is that you rescind that territory at the end of your pitch. This is the fundamental difference between an arrogant pitcher who acts like he owns the place and a confident pitcher who knows that he owns the space.

The space, the right to work within the territory, is a privilege granted by the client. You accept that privilege when you enter the room, and you hand the territory back when you leave. In between those two points, it is your responsibility to take good care of it.

Let's explore a few ways to close your pitch in more detail.

Call to Action

The call to action is the key to your pitch, because it contains the very reason that you are pitching – your outcome.

Think back to Secret One, It's All About Them. What form should your call to action take?

Should it be a simple instruction, like "I want you to make a decision right now to go ahead with this project"?

No. The audience doesn't care what you want. It's all about them, remember?

I know it's paradoxical. You are pitching because you want something, but in order for you to get that you have to give the audience something that they want or need.

Now let's add something in from Secret Five; Features and Benefits.

Your call to action must give the audience a reason to act that is in their interests, and your pitch provides the means to achieve that result. The subject of your pitch, your product or service, is the means by which the client will realise the benefits to them.

Let's say you're pitching for approval for a project. Here's an example call to action

"Support my project and it will save you 20% on costs"

"If you want to save 20% on costs, all you have to do is support my project now"

Closing the Loop

You'll find the description for this in the Opening section of Secret Three, Steady, Ready Pitch, so I won't repeat it. Suffice to say that you close the loop that you opened at the beginning of your pitch.

The Promise

As with Closing the Loop, you'll find the description for this in Secret Three.

You might promise that, by the end of your pitch, someone in the audience will have said a certain phrase. You have to be very confident in your pitch to try this kind of prediction, but it's definitely worthwhile when someone in the audience says, "If only we had bought this product last year..." and you pull the card out of the envelope to reveal those same words.

Thank You

The audience has given you their time and attention, and the least you can do is to acknowledge that with a sincere 'thank you'.

If you're planning an emotive, high impact ending, you might not want to lessen the impact by saying thank you afterwards, so say it before. For example, "I'm grateful for your time and attention today, and in closing I want to remind you that..."

What do comedians and stage performers end with?

"You've been a great audience, thank you and good night!"

Encore!

Have you ever sat in the cinema, watching the closing credits, wondering if there are any funny bits to see, hidden amongst the lists of names?

The 'Airplane' series of spoof disaster movies probably started the trend. Then other films followed with 'out-takes' hidden in the credits. Pixar[8] created 'out-takes' just for that purpose. Other films hide crucial plot twists after the final credits have finished, and you generally find out when you tell someone you saw the film and they ask, "Wow! Did you see the final scene after the credits?" and you realise why you were the only people who left at the end of the film.

Every audience at a rock concert expects an encore. Some performers make the audience wait for up to an hour before being reluctantly coaxed back onto the stage for one more song... or two... or ten.

I wouldn't expect your audience to be shouting "More!" at the end of your pitch. By now, your pitch will be getting very good indeed. It's just that audiences for pitches and presentations tend to express themselves a little differently.

The principle is the same, though.

I've been reading a few websites on the subject of closing a presentation to see what suggestions are out there. The general consensus is to "give the audience something that leaves them begging for more". My first thought was 'Heroin'. I decided that it's probably best that I don't read other peoples' websites after all.

I performed at The Comedy Store in London for twelve years as an

---

8 Interestingly, Pixar have also reinvented the idea of a cartoon preceding the main feature and, in doing so, have reinvigorated the art of animated 'shorts'

improviser and in a couple of different acts. One of them, The Calypso Twins (with Ainsley Harriott; I was the tall black one) had a reputation for being very a hard act to follow, so we usually closed the first half or the entire show. We had a lot of encores but it's sometimes difficult for the audience to call for "More!" when you're half way through the show.

Your audience will metaphorically shout, "More!" by coming up to you at the end of your pitch with questions. If you've been giving an informative presentation, perhaps a lecture or a presentation at a conference, you'll find that the audience want to take away something to remember you by. That's why speakers often sell books and CDs at the back of the lecture room; it's not only because it's a sales opportunity, it's because the audience demands more of the speaker.

What's the encore to your pitch? Do you send a DVD with the video highlights? A 'Best Of' compilation CD? A thank you card? As an absolute minimum, you must send a follow up letter.

Surely, you do something, don't you?

You don't just wave them off and hope for the best, do you?

The seeds that you have planted in your pitch need watering. They need nurturing. Those ideas must be strengthened if they are to flourish into a fully fledged decision, a firm commitment to you and your product or service.

When you wave the client goodbye, all kinds of things can happen. Your competitors can come along and try to influence them. They can get back to the office to discover all kinds of calamities that have landed on their desks in their absence. They can go off on holiday and it just slips their mind. Their manager might want to share his opposing views. They might even forget some of your key points.

Pitching is one, vital step in your sales process, and that process is not over until you see a signature on a contract. Even then it's not over, because when the delivery starts, that is another sales opportunity in itself.

So the pitch starts long before you begin speaking, and it ends long after you close your laptop and the rest of the office staff come in to pick their way through the broken biscuits, dried up sandwiches and wrinkly grapes.

Follow up letters

A follow up letter is perhaps the most important post-pitch activity. As soon as the pitch is complete, make sure you make notes about key events, statements from the client, valuable questions and so on.

If you have been pitching as a team, make notes during the pitch and set an hour aside afterwards to compare notes and create a follow up letter as part of your ongoing strategy, because the pitch isn't over until you get the purchase order, the 'green light', the 'yes' or whatever else your outcome might be.

Use the key points in your follow up letter, and put it in the post on the day of the pitch, if possible. When the client receives the letter the next day, it creates a clear link between your pitch and your desire to work with them.

If you asked a number of suppliers to give you an estimate for some building work, which of these would you favour?

- ☐ One that you have to call after two weeks to get the estimate
- ☐ One that gives you a verbal estimate over the phone but won't put it in writing
- ☐ One that sends a written estimate after two weeks
- ☐ One that sends a written estimate after two days

What impression do you get from each of these?

A hand written follow up letter is rare these days and therefore has added impact. A copy and paste email probably has no benefit at all. It's like getting a letter from a utility provider saying "Dear Homeowner". Think about it. Does it make you feel special?

In your letter, you can include the most important points of your pitch, and if possible, any audience questions or comments. Show them that the letter is about the experience they just had. It serves the same purpose as your holiday photos, jogging your memory about your favourite moments.

If the client has seen pitches from a number of suppliers, your follow up letter will help to make yours stand out.

Imagine that you're interviewing for a job and you see three candidates. They can all do the job and all three seem keen enough. One of them sends you a hand written letter, thanking you for you time and reminding you of why they're the perfect candidate, and even outlining some ideas that they would like to bring to the job.

What impression does that give you?

If you're thinking "creep" then I'm guessing that writing a follow up letter is something you would never do. Why is that?

If you're thinking "they really want the job!" then that's exactly what most interviewers will think.

JM Enterprises
1st January 2010

Dear Tom,

I'm writing to thank you for your time and hospitality on Tuesday when you gave me the opportunity to pitch our proposal for a new mouse trap to you and your team.

We particularly valued your input on the packaging options and your ideas have now been incorporated into our marketing plan for the new design.

I'd like to emphasise what I feel are the most valuable points of our proposal so that I can ensure you have what you need to make the right decision. To work with us would have the following benefits:

We will reduce your time to market by 50%
We will reduce your marketing costs by 20%
We will increase Return On Investment by 30%

If you decide to accept our proposal by Friday, we can be ready to begin work by the following Monday.

I am available to answer whatever questions you and your team may have, and we are all looking forward very much to seeing you again and to working with you.

With best regards,

Jerry

If you think back to Secret Five's embedded commands, do you notice any in this follow up letter?

There's no particular rule for how to write a follow up letter, because each pitch and situation is different.

There are, however, some points that you should always include:

- ☐ A thank you for the audience's time

- ☐ The most important points of your pitch

- ☐ A reminder of what you want the reader to do

- ☐ The next step, should they make a favourable decision

- ☐ A sincere desire to continue building a professional relationship

In fact, if you follow any 'rules' or set format for a follow up letter, it could come across as a 'cut and paste' template, and that will do more harm than good. Compare the example of the follow up letter on the previous page to this one:

TC Enterprises
1st January 2010

Dear Client,

Thank you for your attendance at our recent pitch. It was very nice to see you there.

I trust that you obtained the information you needed from it and I look forward to receiving your decision at your earliest convenience.

I would like to take this opportunity to remind you that TC Enterprises is the leading manufacturer of products to the mouse catching industry, with production facilities in eight countries and an annual turnover in excess of $10,000,000. With local support offices in 26 countries, you can be assured of our personal attention at all times.

Yours Faithfully,

Tom

This letter has a considerable time saving advantage over the previous example, because you can simply print a copy off after any pitch you deliver. However, if your time is that short, you might benefit more by cutting down on the number of pitches you're delivering.

In this age of email and instant messaging, a letter is something special. Your client receives so many emails, on subjects ranging from the trivial to the laughable, that another email just gets lost in the noise. And since most of the letters your client receives are bills and adverts, a personal letter will be very welcome indeed.

A follow up letter is an extension to your pitch. It drives home the key message, keeps your pitch fresh in the clients' mind and creates a bridge to your next meeting.

Even if your pitch is not successful, you can at least expect detailed and objective feedback from the client. Remember that every pitch is an opportunity to learn, and your audience is your best teacher.

Thank You, You've Been a Wonderful Audience

Your pitch began long before you spoke your first word, and it ends long after you have said, "thank you" and closed your laptop.

This brings us to the end of Secret Seven and indeed to the end of the book.

I hope that, as a result of reading this book, you have realised that a pitch is much more than just another presentation. It is a unique opportunity to make a connection with your audience, to claim your space, to convey your hopes and dreams into your client's mind and to lead the audience on a rich, vivid, emotive journey that leads directly to the best result that you could hope for – a successful, fruitful and mutually rewarding business relationship.

The Pitching Bible contains everything that you need in order to make this happen. There's a lot to take in, because a pitch is a complex and deep interaction, once we break it down and really begin to analyse it.

Pitching is complex because people are complex. A single person is complex enough, but when you place a number of them together in a room and call them an audience, they begin to interact and behave in ways that you couldn't have imagined. Yet, overall, they have a compelling need to relate to you and to support you.

Your audience wants you to succeed. Why would they spend their valuable time watching someone fail?

Your audience wants the same thing that you do – to make that connection, to understand your idea and to make a decision that is as good for them as it is for you.

When you're pitching, you and your audience share a unique experience that will never happen again. That pitch, that moment is one of a kind.

Make every moment count. Make every pitch count.

Secret Brief

The End?

The pitch ends when the decision is made, and not before.

Questions

Take questions before you summarize so that you can incorporate them into your closing and maintain control until you've finished.

Why Do People Ask Questions?

It's rarely why you would like them to.

Handling Questions

ERR. Echo, Rephrase, Reply

Anticipating Questions

It's better to answer than to be asked.

Just Five More Minutes.... Pleeeeease

One more question? At your own peril...

Closing Your Pitch

However you close your pitch, the important thing is that you close it. Closing your pitch hands the room back to the audience and completes the marking of your territory.

Encore!

What's your encore? As a minimum, a personalised follow up letter.

Thank You, You've Been a Wonderful Audience

No, really, I mean it. Remember to tip your waitress.

THE 7 SECRETS OF A SUCCESSFUL PITCH

The Seven Secrets

Secret 1: It's All About Them

You can solve any problem in your pitch by looking at it from the audience's point of view. Your outcome is for you, your focus is on your audience.

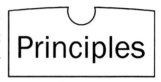

Secret 2: By The Time You Start, It's Already Too Late

When you stand up and open your mouth, you have already missed your chance to influence the audience.

The pitch begins the moment the audience buys the ticket.

Secret 3: Steady, Ready, Pitch

Make sure you have the audience's full attention before you begin, even if you spend most of the time getting it.

Secret 4: Dream The Dream

Your pitch began as an idea, so first put convey those ideas into a vivid, tangible reality within the audience's mind.

Secret 5: Mind Your Language

Make the difference between a good pitch and a winning pitch by carefully crafting your language.

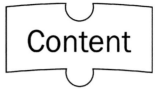

Secret 6: Say It Again, Sam

To make a decision, the client has to go through a process of learning, so understanding the basic principles of learning will make your pitch more memorable and influential.

Secret 7: The End... Or Is It?

The pitch doesn't end when you close your laptop.

The pitch ends when you get the result... the contract, the decision, the 'yes'.

Now you can see how the Seven Secrets of a Successful Pitch fit together, like the pieces of a jigsaw puzzle. Each Secret both builds upon and serves as a foundation for the others.

If you dip into this book, looking for some ideas on how to open your pitch or some tips on how to use stories then you'll certainly find what you're looking for, yet when you build your pitch around all Seven Secrets, the result will be far greater than the sum of its parts.

You may recall that your mind and body are not only a single system, they form a single, seamless system. Your pitch works in exactly the same way, designed from the start as a single, seamless means of getting your message across to your client.

We can assume that, in a competitive market, there isn't a great deal to choose between suppliers. A range of products and services exist across a wide range of prices and different customers are prepared to pay to have their own needs and preferences met.

Therefore, I'm sorry to say that in your price range, your competitors are very similar to you. Their product, service, format or design may have slightly different features or qualities than yours, but that isn't because one is better than the other. It's because, without differences, the customer wouldn't have to choose, which would in turn mean very little leverage for the sales person over and above their personality and ability to build a relationship with the client.

For example, if you compare ten cars from different manufacturers that are in the same size and price range, what is the real difference between them? Style. Personal taste. Brand allegiance. All subjective criteria. 'Budget' manufacturers give higher standard equipment levels to offset a poorer brand image. 'Prestige' manufacturers align their brand values with quality, although their cars are probably no more or less reliable than any other. Industry standards make issues such as safety and economy a level playing field.

When the market is so saturated and so confusing, what does the customer turn to? They buy what they like the look of. And the 'look' of a product perhaps owes more to market positioning that design. Cars are photographed at certain angles, in certain colours, in certain locations. The background of the photo says "city" or "sporty" or "sexy" or "safe". The marketers and advertisers craft a personality that fits with that of the target customer.

The product becomes secondary to the pitch, and the pitch becomes the only way to get your message heard above the background noise of your competitors.

Each of these puzzle pieces takes your core message and elevates it to a position high above that of your competitors.

When you read, learn and apply these Seven Secrets, you give your pitch every chance to be an outstanding success.

Now that I have shared with you the Secrets that it has taken me 25 years to learn, the rest is up to you.

Paul

THE
APPENDIX

Solutions to Puzzles

Secret One

Are the horizontal lines curved or straight?

They're straight. So are these:

And this isn't really moving:

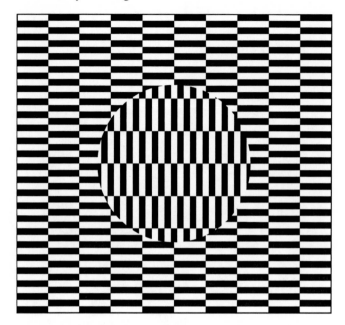

How does this next optical illusion work?

At the back of your eye there is a 'blind spot' where your optic nerve exits the retina. There are no light sensitive cells in this area, and if you look at the full moon at night, that's how big the hole is.

How is it that you don't see a 'hole' in the world? Your visual perception literally 'wallpapers' over the hole by copying and blending in whatever is around the hole, to create the illusion of an uninterrupted field of vision.

Try slowly sliding your finger tip over the face that is in your blind spot. Weird, eh?

I know you're sceptical, so try these versions too.

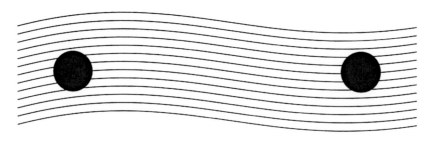

Do you remember that, back in Secret Five, we talked about the phenomenon of losing your car keys or some paperwork when the missing item is right under your nose?

Just think, if your brain can wallpaper over a gaping hole in the back of your retina, what can it do with a set of keys on a table or a piece of missing information from your pitch?

Large items don't get lost in your physical blind spot, but the phenomenon of 'negative hallucination' is just as real.

All of this takes place without your conscious awareness, so the danger is that your pitch is missing something vital, and you don't even know it.

Have you ever walked into a room and not been able to remember why you went in there? Have you hesitated at your front door, certain you've forgotten something but unable to remember what it is until it's just too late to go back for it?

This is why it's so important to prepare your pitch with a friend or colleague. They can see what you can't see and can point out things that might be hiding in your blind spot.

Are the table tops the same size?

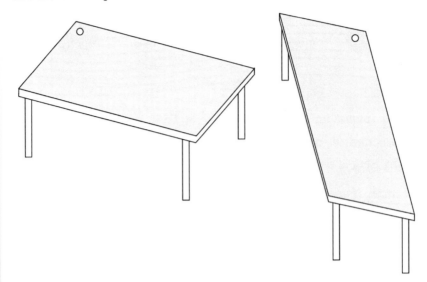

Yes, exactly the same.

The illusion of perspective makes them look like they're different tables seen from the same angle instead of the same table seen from different angles.

Measure them and find out for yourself. The circle is in the same corner on both 'table tops' to help you measure them accurately. They are the same image, just rotated by 90 degrees and with legs moved to provide the correct perspective.

Secret Three

From BOAT to FISH, changing only one letter at a time. Can you do it in fewer than 10 steps?

B   O   A   T

B   E   A   T

B   E   S   T

B   U   S   T

B   U   S   H

B   A   S   H

M   A   S   H

M   A   S   T

F   A   S   T

F   I   S   T

F   I   S   H

Secret Six

Spot the Difference

When you looked at this image, the cells in your retinas responded initially to the change in light levels reflecting from the paper. As you continued to look at the image, the light levels didn't change, and if you held your gaze very still, the nerves in your retinas became 'tired'.

When you then looked at a white surface, the difference in light levels made a negative image appear, and you would have seen something like the pleasing image on the left.

You can try this yourself if you have some photo editing software on your computer.

Try it with a colour image too; just convert the image to a 'negative', stare at it on your computer screen for twenty seconds and then look at a white wall or a sheet of paper.

Because white light is a mixture of other colours of light, you will see the colours the right way round again. The optical illusion works in colour because the negative colours are subtracted from the white light reflecting off the paper, leaving the correct colours.

You can even test that this is a function of your retina and not the visual cortex in your brain by looking at the image with only one eye. When you then look at the white surface, alternate eyes and you'll see that the effect only happens with the eye that you used to stare at the image.

Memory Labels

Read the whole exercise out to ten people.

How many of them thought about Christmas?

Why do you think that is?

Copyright

This is relevant for you if you are pitching creative ideas.

Unfortunately, you can't copyright an idea. You can copyright the expression of an idea – a script or design, perhaps – but you can't protect the idea itself. If you could, you would have a monopoly on ideas, which a judge would never grant.

Two different studios can release films about the same subject, and a million different songwriters can all write about love, as long as they don't copy another songwriter's exact words or melody.

If. at the end of your pitch, the client says, "that's a great idea", they may be up to more than just complimenting you. They may be carefully defining what you just pitched as an idea, and therefore something that you can't copyright.

The polite response might be "thank you", but the wise response would be "I appreciate you saying that you like my unique work, are you saying that you want to buy it?"

By acknowledging the client's assertion that your pitch was an 'idea', you have acknowledged that your 'idea' can't be protected.

In copyright law, you have to prove originality and one of the simplest ways to do this is to post a securely sealed copy of your material to yourself using a tracked mail service. Don't open the package when it arrives, just put it in a safe place.

If you ever need to, take your unopened package along to court, open it in front of the judge and show the contents as the original which you are seeking to protect. The postmark on the package and the date on the delivery tracking information prove the date on which the material was in existence, which is why it's important that the package is securely sealed.

Bibliography and Recommended Reading

Structure of Magic, Volumes 1 & 2, Richard Bandler & John Grinder

Conversations, Dr Richard Bandler & Owen Fitzpatrick

Using Your Brian for a Change, Richard Bandler

My Voice Will Go With You, Sydney Rosen

Quantum Psychology, Robert Anton Wilson

Frogs into Princes, Richard Bandler & John Grinder

Persuasion Engineering, Richard Bandler & John LaValle

In Praise of Slow, Carl Honore

Man's Search for Meaning, Victor Frankl

Everybody Poops, Taro Gomi

Paul Boross

Paul Boross is an internationally recognised authority on pitching to influence in business critical situations.

As the business world becomes ever more competitive, the ability to capture clients' attention and pitch to win is even more vital, and Paul's expertise in pitching has earned him the reputation of 'The Pitch Doctor', helping CEOs, politicians, business leaders and sales teams in companies such as Google, the BBC, the Financial Times, RBS, MTV and JP Morgan.

Paul is probably the world's only presentations/pitch specialist, business trainer and life change expert to have real front-line experience of both motivational psychology and high profile television/stage presentation and comedy.

As an authority in communications, presentation, performance and pitching skills, Paul has coached and developed a large number of leading media business people, politicians and performers in the art and science of 'getting the message across'. He is also a respected keynote speech writer and performance coach for many top business, professional, political and entertainment clients, including Sir Richard Branson and Dermot Murnaghan.

Paul's achievements encompass prime time TV, business success, chart topping hit records, and transforming the lives of thousands of people with his unique brand of motivational psychology. He is an internationally renowned business trainer, media commentator and advisor to film stars, music moguls, business leaders and politicians around the globe.

Paul regularly lectures all over the world for The Entertainment Masterclasses and media festivals such as MIP, MIPCOM, BCWW, Kristallen and Edinburgh.

Television and radio credits

- Presented the primetime BBC2 series Speed Up Slow Down, which focused on time management and psychology.

- Motivational psychologist on Sky's series School of Hard Knocks with Will Greenwood.

- Appeared in ITV's Wannabe, advising young people on the psychology of breaking into the TV and the music businesses.

- Appearances in BBC1's The Politics Show.

- Regular contributor to Radio Five Live, LBC and BBC Radio London.

Music and comedy credits

- Headline act at London's The Comedy Store, where he performed for over 12 years.

- Founded, with Tony Hawks, the comedy band Morris Minor and The Majors, whose number-one hits included Stutter Rap and This Is The Chorus.

- One half of the comedy singing duo The Calypso Twins with Ainsley Harriott, which had a major hit with World Party.

- Regular guest appearances with The Comedy Store Players on improvisation nights (with Paul Merton and Josie Lawrence, among others).

- Trained with Mike Myers (Saturday Night Live; Wayne's World; Austin Powers) in advanced improvisation skills.

Training qualifications

- ☐ Licensed Trainer in Neuro-Linguistic Programming (Society of NLP)

- ☐ Licensed Master Practitioner of Neuro-Linguistic Programming (Society of NLP)

- ☐ Licensed Practitioner of Neuro-Linguistic Programming (Society of NLP)

- ☐ Licensed NLP Hypnosis Practitioner (SNLP)

- ☐ Licensed Health Practitioner of Neuro-Linguistic Programming (NLP)

- ☐ Diploma in Teaching Excellence (Matrix)

- ☐ Diploma in the Application of Direct and Indirect Hypnosis in Consultation and Treatment (SOMNLP)

- ☐ Licensed Practitioner of Persuasion Engineering (SNLP)

- ☐ Diploma in Life Coaching (Newcastle College)

- ☐ PhD in Meta Physics (ULC California)

- ☐ Certificate in Coaching Mastery (Michael Neil; Genius Catalyst)

- ☐ UK Athletics Licensed Coach

- ☐ Medical NLP Trainer (Guy's Hospital, Kings College Hospital, St Thomas' Hospital (GKT)

The Pitch Doctor

The Pitch Doctor has one mission: to help you win business.

How? By coaching you in the art and science of pitching. By showing you how to present yourself, your company and your product to optimal effect. By equipping you with a tool kit of psychology, NLP, performance, communication and storytelling techniques that not only deliver commercial results, but build relationships and keep clients coming back for more.

Paul Boross is probably the world's only presentations/pitch specialist, business trainer and personal change expert to have real front-line experience of both motivational psychology and high profile television/stage presentation and comedy.

Paul is an internationally renowned expert on the art of pitching. With dozens of TV, radio and stage credits, and after working with CEOs, politicians, business leaders and sales teams in companies such as Google, the BBC, the Financial Times, RBS and JP Morgan, he has earned his reputation as 'The Pitch Doctor'.

It's not the taking part that counts in today's ruthless marketplace; it's the winning. The Pitch Doctor tips the balance in your favour, giving you a real and tangible competitive edge.

The symptoms

Your clients can't buy from call centres or brochures – they need to look you in the eye and know that they can rely on you. In an increasingly competitive and commoditised marketplace, the client is buying a relationship. Products no longer differentiate – people do.

You might find that you're not winning as many pitches as you feel you should, given your brand or product fit, and you might even get feedback from clients that your pitching team didn't seem to really want the business.

The more effort you put into creating presentations and arming your sales teams with the best information, the further away they seem to get from making that genuine connection with a client and, most importantly, winning the business.

The diagnosis

Pitching — the art of getting your message across — is one of the most important skills in your tool kit. But it is also one of the least understood. All too often the process is rushed, the participants unprepared and the outcome unsatisfactory.

Most people aren't natural-born "pitchers". It's a skill — like driving a car — that needs to be acquired and continually refined.

Combining psychological insight with a lifetime of pitching skills and a dose of commercial instinct, The Pitch Doctor will show you how to put across your message in a way that does you, and your product, credit. He and his team will cut through the clutter, differentiate your offer, and give you what you need to drive the client's decision process.

A lost pitch is not just a missed opportunity; it's a waste of time, effort and investment. It strengthens your competitors, takes time away from the business you could win and moves you further away from your goals. By the time you stand up to pitch, you should already know how you're going to win the business.

The prescription

Winning is a state of mind. While a good pitch isn't going to save a bad product, a bad pitch can kill a good one.

It's not always the best companies or the most innovative products that are the most successful; it's the best pitched.

Most pitches attempt to tune in to their audience using one or two channels, such as pictures or words. But the best pitches resonate on all frequencies: emotional, intellectual, visual, verbal. If you hit all these touch points — if you can make your audience see, hear and feel your message — you have a 100% greater chance of selling them your product.

But don't take our word for it.

The Pitch Doctor's clients report up to a 75% increase in their pitch success rate following a consultation.

Which is just what the doctor ordered.

The Treatment

Whether you're preparing for a single, critical pitch, developing your client facing teams to pitch more effectively or even making sure that your media facing executives get the right message across, The Pitch Doctor is the answer.

Pitch Coaching

When everything rests on getting a single pitch right, with no margin for error, The Pitch Doctor will work with you to plan and prepare. Offering you honest and even ruthless feedback before the pitch, and the tools to get back on track, you're in a far stronger position than if you hope for the best and wait for the client's feedback. If you drop the ball in front of the client, there are no second chances.

The Pitch Doctor's coaching service is tailored precisely to your needs and, simply, makes the difference between getting close and winning easily.

Team Development

When your sales teams are pitching regularly and their success rate simply isn't where it needs to be, you are losing money. Pitching is time consuming and, most importantly, your reputation hinges on it. A missed opportunity not only takes your focus away from business you could have won, it strengthens your competitors too.

The Pitch Doctor's team development programs are uniquely designed for your culture, your clients and your needs to ensure you make the most of every opportunity to connect with your clients.

Media Coaching

The Pitch Doctor's unique blend of broadcast experience and personal coaching expertise gives your media facing executives a unique means to hone their presentation delivery skills, develop their confidence and charisma and send the right message to clients and shareholders.

Perfect Pitch

A written proposal or pitch document makes an important impression on your clients which lasts long after the pitch itself. The Pitch Doctor's proposal review service gives you the opportunity to refine your written message in exactly the same way as with one to one Pitch Coaching, enabling you to make the right impression and get the client's attention, every time.

Big Sky

Big Sky offers global training for exceptional performance and integrated learning solutions.

We inspire businesses across a wide range of sectors by the education and transformation of their people.

Our team of highly professional trainers and executive coaches have more than 60 years of combined experience in training individuals and organisations. We put the emphasis on experiential learning through entertaining courses.

We help leaders and their teams become more effective, more productive and more focused by creating the high performance mindset needed to succeed.

Our trainers and coaches are chosen for their integrity, professionalism and humour. They all come from a successful and diverse business background so that they can immediately establish the respect of course participants and truly lead by example.

The Big Sky values are communication, passion, integrity, achievement, service, growth, support, humour, continuous learning, commitment, excellence and fun.

We provide corporate training which:

□ Targets six key business skills that guarantee success

□ Helps you capitalise on your core strengths in a tough marketplace

□ Is delivered by expert practitioners armed with current best practice

When the landscape is constantly changing, only those with the ability to adapt will thrive. Big Sky's distinctive training is designed to strengthen and sharpen six core business skills that can get you through even the most hostile environment - towards a wider, brighter, breath-taking horizon.

When times are tough it takes everything you've got just to keep up, just to survive. By strengthening your core business competencies we'll help you see your marketplace with new eyes and make the most of where you are right now.

Ever picked your way through dense forest or driven along a narrow mountain pass? You turn a corner, suddenly the darkness falls away and the sky just opens up in front of you. Big Sky delivers training that gives you the same sense of liberation, exhilaration and optimism.

Reclaim your horizons with Big Sky.

Training that explores you

If you're simply following the road ahead, the chances are someone got there before you. That's why Big Sky carves out a new and unique learning path for you. We work to understand you, we question, we listen, we find out where you are and where you'd rather be. Your business and your people are unique, so why isn't your training program unique yet?

Coaching that focuses you

During periods of extreme cold, the human body survives by diverting blood supply to its core organs. In tough times, smart leaders dedicate resources to the development of core business skills. The ones that truly change the way people work together, improving communication, increasing motivation, enhancing confidence and driving performance:

Expertise that surprises you

Our coaches are experts. Not dusty experts with piles of books behind them but busy, hands-on experts who are still working at the coalface with businesses every day. Experts who will show you today's best practice not yesterday's. Vibrant, motivational experts with a big sense of humour and an ability to communicate so you feel and enjoy and remember what you're learning. Experts with experience, anecdotes and case studies that will make you say "I see!" like no other training course ever did.

- ☐ Communication and People Skills
- ☐ Presentation Skills
- ☐ Sales and Marketing
- ☐ Leadership
- ☐ Team Development
- ☐ Personal Development
- ☐ Project/Time Management
- ☐ Specialist courses

The Consulting Room

Visit www.thepitchingbible.com for more ideas and for resources that you can download and use when you're preparing your pitches.

The checklists mentioned in this book can be found by visiting the website's secure area, which you can access by registering your name and email address.

Once you've done that, you'll be able to access more information and get the latest updates from The Pitch Doctor including special offers and invitations, insider information and The Pitch Doctor's consulting room where you can ask questions and get the latest tips and hints from The Pitch Doctor.

Contacting The Pitch Doctor

You can contact The Pitch Doctor by email at:

info@thepitchdoctor.tv

Checklists

You can also download these from www.thepitchingbible.com

Videos

You can find video tutorials at: www.thepitchingbible.com

Lightning Source UK Ltd.
Milton Keynes UK

176317UK00003B/4/P